Churchill in the Trenches

PETER APPS

ISBN: 10-1517752434
ISBN-13: 978-1517752439

DEDICATION

To those at the tip of the spear

CONTENTS

ACKNOWLEDGMENTS

As always, many thanks to Amazon for the opportunity. To my long suffering carers Gabrielle and Melanie for turning pages on some of the documents and to my Project for Study of the 21st Century chief of staff Claire for taking some of my dictation.

PETER APPS

Introduction

The commandeered former London bus set them down in a shattered, shell-scarred town. There were close to three miles still to go, they were told, and they would have to walk it.

They were the headquarters element of the 6th Battalion Royal Scots Fusiliers. Their unit had been amongst the first of the volunteers to join at the outbreak of war. Now, in January 1916, most of the old faces had gone.

Many of them had lasted less than six months after their arrival in France in May the previous year. At the end of September, the battalion had fought its first pitched battle in the body-strewn trenches of Loos. It had lost all but two of its officers and a sizeable portion of its men.

It wasn't the first time on the Ypres Salient, the fields around what had once been a picturesque medieval Belgian market town. A spell less than a month earlier, amid the clinging mud and petrified trees known as Sanctuary Wood, had also cost them comrades.

This time, they were heading for the village of Ploegsteert—"Plugstreet" to the British Toms. No-one particularly liked the idea.

For the more experienced soldiers there, what they now simply called the War must have felt a living nightmare. All were volunteers—conscription would not come until later in the year. Most would have grown up in the countryside, all of them born before the invention of the airplane. Few would have seen more than a handful of motorcars or vehicles before they came to France.

One man, however, almost seemed to be enjoying himself.

The new commander had spent several weeks training the battalion, trying to win them over—but many still had doubts. He had replaced a man they liked and trusted.

The lieutenant colonel turned to one of his captains. While most of the men wore the distinctive peaked cap of the British Army, this man wore a French-issue metal helmet. In the gloom, it was almost enough to break up the profile of one of the best-known men in Europe.

"Here we are," he said, absentmindedly in his unmistakable growl. "Here we are, torn away from the Senate and the Forum to fight in the battlefields of France."

The officer he spoke to—a peacetime Edinburgh lawyer—scarcely replied.

Like many of the men, he was beginning to wonder whether the new CO was ever so slightly mad.

As the detachment arrived, one of the guides escorting the Fusiliers turned to the former lawyer.

"Excuse me, sir," he said. "But your commanding officer is very like Mr. Winston Churchill."

BY THE TIME he arrived in Flanders at the end of 1915, Britain's future leader was at perhaps the most difficult point in his life.

For most of the last four years, he had been First Lord of the Admiralty, the senior Cabinet minister responsible for whole swathes of Imperial maritime strategy.

He had also found himself blamed for one of the greatest fiascos of the war so far: the Dardanelles. What Churchill had touted as a quick way to turn the course of the war through attacking Turkey had turned into a costly disaster.

Churchill always maintained he did nothing wrong, that the strategy was a reasonable risk undermined by colleagues who gave it inadequate resourcing. But he felt destroyed. "I am finished," he told his friends.

Forty-one years old, he had already been a legend for almost two decades, first as a reporter, then in politics. Now he was placing himself alongside ordinary soldiers at the heart of the conflict. Everyone knew he might be killed. Not everyone believed he cared.

Churchill's five months at the front were more than just an interlude. For a man born into the aristocracy in Blenheim Palace who lived a life of prestige and luxury, they were perhaps his most extended sojourn amongst ordinary people.

They were his most prolonged exposure to the grinding nature of everyday war. He had fought before, of course, in South Africa, Sudan, on the northwest Frontier. But none of those experiences had been in any way typical.

Rather than part of the conventional military chain of command, he had been a war correspondent. The trenches were different.

Churchill—author of several dozen books chronicling not just his life but his ancestors and his era—barely wrote of his time in the trenches. His experiences there were granted only a handful of paragraphs in "The World Crisis," his epic history of the Great War. Two essays written in the 1920s barely scratched the surface of his experience.

But there is no shortage of detail. One of his officers, Andrew Dewar Gibb—the captain of the introduction—wrote his own account between the wars. There is the battalion's war diary, a smattering of other accounts from soldiers who were there.

There are Churchill's own letters, mainly to his desperately worried wife Clementine.

They provide a fascinating portrait of a man trying to hold himself and his men together under sometimes hugely challenging conditions. Under his command, the battalion might never have fought a major battle but it was under frequent shellfire, living in desperately grim conditions and suffering no

shortag
e of dead and wounded.

Maintaining grip and leadership under such circumstances, he told his officers, was as much an act as anything else.

"War is a game played with a smile," he said repeatedly. "If you can't smile, grin. If you can't grin, stay out of the way until you can."

He turned up in the trenches with a phenomenal array of extras, from hampers to wine to an improbably large bathtub. But he shared and won the men over.

Another junior officer, Jock McDavid, an initial skeptic, later said: "After a very brief period he had accelerated the morale of officers and men to an almost unbelievable degree. It was sheer personality."

His finest hour, of course, was yet to come.

PETER APPS

Chapter 1 – A Rise and Fall

Shortly after Britain declared war on August 4, 1914, the Prime Minister's wife, Margot Asquith, saw Churchill striding through the Downing Street corridors. The most striking thing about him, she wrote that night in her diary, was his "happy face."

Our image of Churchill is now so bound up with the Second World War that it is easy to forget that, at the time, he clearly felt 1914 was the moment history had shaped him for. And as First Lord of the Admiralty since October 1911, he believed he had helped prepare the country for it.

Always a workaholic, he had thrown himself into the job. In his three peacetime years in the role, he spent a total of five months out visiting the fleet on his personal Admiralty yacht. He spent most of his weekends on warships and bases. While most of the world believed the arms race with Germany would end peacefully, he expected war from the beginning.

In July 1914 as Europe's powers mobilized following the assassination of Austrian Archduke Franz Ferdinand, Churchill wrote to his wife that his sheer enthusiasm for the crisis worried him.

"Everything tends towards catastrophe and collapse," he wrote. "I am interested, geared up and happy—is it not horrible to be built like that?"

Other observers took a slightly more generous line.

"Let me not be supposed to imply that Churchill was working for war or desired it," Foreign Secretary Sir Edward Grey wrote in his memoirs. "It was only that his high-metalled sprit was exhilarated by the air of crisis."

FROM HIS EARLIEST days, Churchill had been fascinated by conflict. Years later, he remembered that the only meaningful conversation he ever enjoyed with his father Randolph took place over his display of model soldiers.

"For years I thought my father...had discerned in me the qualities of military genius," Churchill wrote in 1930. "But I was later told that he had only come to the conclusion that I was not clever enough to go to the Bar [to train as a lawyer]."

In his last three years at Harrow School, the young Winston was put in the "Army Class," the group preparing themselves for entry to the Royal Military Academy Sandhurst.

Never regarded as hugely academic despite his passion for history, Churchill failed his first two attempts at the entry exam. Accepted at the third attempt, he received a cavalry cadetship—less academically demanding than the infantry. In 1896, he was commissioned into the 4th Hussars and sailed for India.

Despite his aristocratic background—he was descended from the Dukes of Marlborough and born in Blenheim Palace—Churchill himself was far from rich. Life as a young officer in a peacetime cavalry regiment was remarkably expensive. His pay was £150 a month—rising to £300 in India—but he needed another £500 to keep himself living in the "style of the regiment."

Churchill's letters to his mother made it clear he wanted her to use her influence to get him nearer to the action.

His first exposure came in Cuba. Local rebels were fighting the Spanish and Churchill managed to get himself attached to their forces as an observer. He spent his twenty-first birthday being shot at, an achievement he regarded as a considerable success.

Back in India, a punitive expedition was being prepared against the Pathan tribesmen of the Swat Valley. Having previously buttonholed its commander at a country house party, Churchill got himself attached as an embedded reporter.

For a young man struggling financially, it was a considerable gamble. Churchill had to travel for five weeks at his own expense to get to the front. But by the end of the year, he had an 85,000-word book out on the subject.

It was an unorthodox approach to a military career. By mid-1898, it was clear he was being noticed—but not always liked.

As he prepared to lead an expedition to Sudan, General Herbert Kitchener initially refused to let the young reporter accompany the force at all. Eventually, and reluctantly, he relented.

"The whole contretemps is a good example of the animosity which, for the first half of his life, his combination of brash bravery and publicity seeking was capable of arousing," wrote Roy Jenkins, one of his many biographers.

On September 2, 1898, Churchill took part in one of the last great cavalry charges at the Battle of Omdurman. Three Victoria Crosses were won and both sides suffered heavy losses.

By early October, he was back in England working on another book. In South Africa, the Boer

War was brewing. Churchill, however, was discovering new ambitions. By early the following year, he was standing for the Conservative Party in his first parliamentary election.

He lost. But it was becoming clearer than ever that a conventional military career was not what he was looking for.

In South Africa, Churchill was once again in uniform. As in Sudan, however, he was more correspondent than soldier, getting himself attached to whichever force he felt most likely to provide good copy. Already a minor celebrity, he was probably the best-paid journalist out there.

On one of his first forays towards the front, he accompanied an armored train. It was ambushed. On the morning of November 15, 1899, he was captured.

As soon as he had the chance, he climbed over the prison fence and fled. Even half a century later, some officers complained that in doing so he prevented others from going ahead with their longer preplanned escapes.

He remained in South Africa another six months, taking part in several more actions, and was amongst the first British troops into both Ladysmith and Pretoria.

Churchill landed at Southampton on July 20, 1900. Two weeks later he was elected Member of Parliament for Oldham. He was twenty-six.

IN 1904, CHURCHILL crossed the floor and defected to the Liberal party. The official reason, he said, was that he felt much closer to the left of center

Liberals when it came to his social conscience. In reality, he had little or no experience of everyday life.

In 1910, the Liberals won in a landslide. The charismatic young turncoat MP—now representing the Scottish town of Dundee—was a political star.

New Prime Minister Henry Herbert Asquith invited him to the Cabinet, offering him the Irish Office. Churchill wrote back and bluntly asked for something more senior, either the Admiralty or Home Office. "It is fitting, if you will allow me to say so, that ministers should occupy positions in the government that correspond to some extent with their influence in the country," he wrote.

Asquith—who had already been well on his way to the top of British politics when he first met Churchill when the latter was awaiting entry to Sandhurst—must have thought him insufferably arrogant. But he made him Home Secretary, the youngest to hold the position since Robert Peel in 1822.

Churchill reveled in his newfound authority. One of the more archaic duties of the Home Secretary was to write a daily letter to the King to update him on parliamentary business. They were chatty, almost gossipy—clearly not the work of a man who knew his station.

He was not an unthinking minister. In particular, he agonized over decisions on which death sentences should be commuted and which carried out.

His reputation, however, remained often one for rash opportunism.

In January 1911, an armed standoff developed in Sidney Street in London's East End. Two armed members of an anarchist gang suspected of a string of robberies and the killing of a policeman were pinned down by several hundred officers.

Churchill raced to the scene accompanied by a detachment of Scots Guards. When the building caught fire, the fire brigade commander asked Churchill whether his men should go in. He told them to let it burn.

"He was perceived as a trigger happy boy scout or a junior officer who wished to behave in the streets of London as though he was still in the Makaland field force or the armoured train in Natal," wrote biographer Jenkins.

When the Admiralty became clear later that year, Asquith seemed glad to move him.

Technically speaking, the Admiralty role was a slight demotion from Home Secretary. But for Churchill the timing was ideal.

Even before being appointed, Churchill was spending ever more of his time on foreign and military affairs. In 1911, he wrote a long and detailed memo to the Committee of Imperial Defence outlining his thoughts on large scale European war.

It was a remarkably prescient document. It posited a German invasion of France and Belgium that all but overwhelmed their defenders until a British military expeditionary force could be sent to hold the line.

Maintaining Britain's naval edge became something of an obsession. Under his direction, the entire Royal Navy was converted from coal to oil power. Lines of new Dreadnaught and Superdreadnaught battleships were laid down.

When war came, he was one of the few

Cabinet officials not out of his depth.

"I can't help but be fond of him," Asquith wrote in October 1914. "He is so resourceful and undismayed, two of the qualities I like best."

Asquith and Churchill clearly fascinated and frustrated each other in almost equal measure. Churchill's political future, Asquith wrote, was amongst the most interesting questions in British politics. On a day-to-day basis, however, he could be insufferable.

"We had a cabinet meeting of three hours, two and a quarter of which was occupied by Winston," Asquith wrote the same month.

Churchill was clearly a regular conversation topic in the Prime Minister's household. Asquith's daughter Violet was a particular admirer—indeed, there were rumors she had attempted suicide after Churchill became engaged to future wife Clementine.

While broadly supportive in public, Churchill privately expressed his doubts about the Prime Minister. In particular, he wrote, he worried over Asquith's nighttime drinking.

CHURCHILL EXERCISED MORE direct control over the Admiralty than any minister before him. He would often send orders to individual ships or formations. The professional head of the Royal Navy at the time, First Sea Lord Prince Louis of Battenberg, seemed happy for him to do so.

The first major setback came within days of the outbreak. The German battlecruiser *Goeben* and cruiser *Breslau* slipped by the British Mediterranean fleet to Turkey. The German government made a gift of them to the Ottoman Empire, effectively bringing

Turkey into the war and humiliating British commanders.

Churchill and his admirals had hoped the British Grand Fleet would quickly smash its German counterpart. The German High Seas Fleet, however, remained in port while its submarines picked off British shipping.

The ground conflict in Europe, meanwhile, was fast bogging down in the stalemate of trench warfare.

By October, Asquith was noting in his diary that Churchill's attention was shifting back to the land campaign. For the first time in more than a decade, many suspected he wished he were back in uniform.

IN THE FIRST week of October, the Belgian government revealed it was likely to surrender the crucial port of Antwerp in the face of an overwhelming German offensive. Churchill "without reluctance" accepted the task of heading there to see what was going on.

He swept around Antwerp in a yachting cap, flitting between the firing line and luxury as he organized British and Belgian forces. "Twenty minutes in a motorcar…and we were back in one of the best hotels in Europe," he wrote after visiting a detachment to Royal Marines.

Barely thirty-six hours after arriving, Churchill telegraphed Asquith suggesting he resign from the Admiralty to take over—with the necessary military rank—the defense of the city.

Kitchener—the old general and Churchill's former Sudan commander now servicing as Secretary of State for War—offered to make Churchill a lieutenant general. The cabinet, however, refused.

A career military officer, General Rawlinson—like many senior officers, one of Churchill's contemporaries from Sudan—was sent instead. Churchill returned to London just as his wife gave birth to their daughter Sarah. Clementine, not unreasonably, told Winston that he had lost all sense of proportion.

Already, his thoughts were turning to another military operation, one he felt could turn the entire course of the war.

AS WAS HIS tradition by now, four days before the start of 1915, Churchill sent Asquith his New Year's letter of advice on how the country, and now of course the war, should be run.

He offered two big ideas. The first, an invasion of Schleswig-Holstein, was a massive undertaking that would have taken the fight to the heart of Germany. The second was scarcely less ambitious: to force passage of the Dardanelles, enter the Black Sea, and hit the central powers from below.

The idea swiftly consumed Churchill. But at the Admiralty, Churchill was now facing much more opposition to his views.

With his German accent and name, Prince Louis Von Battenberg had become untenable as First Sea Lord. His replacement was Jackie Fisher, one of Britain's most legendary admirals and architect—with Churchill—of much of its naval rebuilding.

The seventy-four-year-old Fisher had first become First Sea Lord in 1904 before retiring six years later. He had been champing at the bit ever since, a constant adviser to Churchill from the outbreak of war onwards. The two men had an intense mutual fascination with each other. But the Royal Navy, it swiftly became clear, was not big enough for two such oversized egos.

Within weeks, the relationship was in tatters. In preparing the Dardanelles camp, Churchill's micromanagement was extreme—sometimes detailing the movement of individual artillery pieces.

"You are just simply eaten up with the Dardanelles and cannot think of anything else!" the old admiral complained to Churchill in one of his trademark letters festooned with capital letters and exclamation marks. "Damn the Dardanelles! They'll be our grave!"

Fisher was in the midst of a growing mental breakdown. But he was not entirely wrong.

The first attempt to force the straits with a flotilla of warships was unsuccessful, blocked by mines and Turkish forts. Two British warships, the *Inflexible* and *Irrepressible*, were lost.

The following landings with ground troops did little better. Allied soldiers—many from the Australia and New Zealand Army Corps (ANZACs)—fought their way ashore only to be pinned down on exposed hillsides and beaches. Within days, the campaign intended to break the deadlock in the European trenches had wound up in exactly the same situation.

Through June, July, and August they slogged on, but with little success. In total, the Allies lost some 56,000 killed, 124,000 wounded, and 7,600 prisoners. That did not include the toll from disease.

The Turks lost similar numbers. But they retained control.

The political fallout was devastating, not least because of the lurid reporting of young Australian journalist Keith Murdoch, father of modern media titan Rupert.

To the end of his life, Churchill maintained he had been justified in pushing forward the Dardanelles operation. It had, he said, at least a reasonable chance of success. And he always denied that it risked undermining the war in Europe by pulling too many troops away. Still, he was the man who had expended almost all his political capital to push it through—and he inevitably paid the price.

"He thought he was finished," his wife Clementine told his official biographer Martin Gilbert decades later. "I thought he would never get over the Dardanelles. I thought he would die of grief."

Amongst the dead was Jack Milbanke, Churchill's closest school friend from Harrow. A lieutenant colonel commanding a battalion of the Sherwood Rangers, he was killed leading a futile charge to break out of the beachhead.

FOR CHURCHILL AND the wider government it all fell apart in mid-May, long before the end of the Dardanelles campaign.

For a brief moment, things were looking promising. While some warships had been withdrawn, there was talk of reinforcements. Then Fisher resigned, disappearing from sight entirely and going into hiding at the Charing Cross Hotel.

It was classic Fisher. But it only served to highlight just how Churchill had failed to work with him.

The Liberal government was already on the brink of collapse. Asquith decided he must approach the Conservatives for a coalition. Churchill—hated by the Conservatives ever since his defection—was now deeply vulnerable.

Asquith asked Churchill if he would take a new role in government or if he would prefer a military command in France. For the first time, Churchill realized he faced losing the Admiralty job.

Churchill seemed to be clutching at straw. On May 17, he raced from Downing Street to the Admiralty building on the merest suggestion the German fleet might be about to sail into the North Sea. But it wasn't—and his time was up.

According to friends, Clementine was visibly upset at the thought of her husband losing his role. She wrote to Asquith: "Winston may in your eyes and those with whom he has to work have faults, but he has the supreme quality which I venture to say very few of your present or future Cabinet possess—the power, the imagination, the deadliness to fight Germany,"

Asquith was having none of it. On May 21, Churchill himself sent a six-page letter. It's not clear it was even read.

When the new government was finally announced on May 26, Churchill had become the Chancellor of the Duchy of Lancaster. He retained his Cabinet rank, but it was an almost meaningless role. In the five months in which he held it, he did not have cause to make a single speech to the House of Commons.

He took a country house for the summer and, for the first time in his life, tried his hand at painting.

It was a hobby he would take with him to the trenches. But despite his periodic protestations to the contrary, his sense of guilt was all too apparent.

"There is more blood than paint upon these hands," he told poet and diplomat Wilfred Scawen Blunt. Blunt later wrote that he believed it was only the painting and Clementine that kept him from losing his mind altogether.

From the sidelines, Churchill continued to lobby for resources for the faltering Dardanelles landings. In July he nearly went there himself to consult with local commanders. But a clear self-destructive tone had entered his writings.

"I shall, of course, be sure to take no unnecessary risks," he wrote to Asquith. "But it will not be possible for me to appreciate the situation without myself landing on the Gallipoli peninsula and in consequence coming under fire. If any mischance should occur, I consider that my wife should receive the pension for a general officer's widow, and I rely on you to see to this."

He went so far as to write a letter to be given to Clementine in the event of his death. His top priority, it seemed, was that his reputation might be rehabilitated.

"There is no hurry, but someday I should like the truth to be known," he wrote, asking her to make sure his Admiralty papers were released. "Do not grieve for me too much... death is only an incident, and not the most important which happens to us in this state of being. On the whole, especially since I met you my darling one I have been happy and you have taught me how mobile a woman's heart can be. If there is anywhere else I shall be on the lookout for you. Meanwhile look forward, feel free, rejoice in life, cherish the children, guard my memory. God bless you. Goodbye. W."

The trip never happened. By October, the withdrawal was underway. Churchill was still writing to the Prime Minister with ideas for grand strategy, but no one was listening.

On November 12, he wrote Asquith a letter of resignation. "I am an officer and I place myself unreservedly at the disposal of the military authorities, observing that my regiment is in France," he wrote.

On Monday, November 15, Churchill made his farewell speech to the House of Commons. Much was taken up with criticizing his enemies, particularly Fisher. It was, critics felt, in parts quite petty. On the wider theme of the war, however, his rhetoric was broader.

"There is no reason to be discouraged about the progress of the war," he said. "We are passing through a bad time, it will probably be worse before it is better. But that it will be better if we only endure and persevere, I have no doubt."

In 1940, such sentiments would inspire a nation. For now, however, few were listening.

He still had his eye on a major command. In a last letter to Asquith he suggested he go to Africa as a commander in chief—presumably a lieutenant general. It's not clear if there was a reply.

On the morning of November 18, 1915, he crossed the Channel.

Chapter 2 – With the Grenadiers

Churchill landed in France in the uniform of a major in the Queen's Own Oxfordshire Hussars (QOOH). It was, quite literally, his family regiment.

Founded in 1818 by his ancestor Francis Spencer Churchill, it was a yeomanry regiment, made up of part-time cavalry drawn from the local area, particularly the staff at Blenheim Palace. It paraded and exercised on the Palace grounds.

Churchill himself had joined in 1902, shortly after his election as MP. As First Lord of the Admiralty, he had ensured they were the first territorial reservist unit to see action, sending them to Flanders as part of the Royal Naval Brigade.

By late 1915, however, the stagnated battlefields were rarely a place for cavalry action. The QOOH was spending spells in the trenches as regular infantry and the rest of the time in reserve, waiting for a breakthrough that never came.

In the weeks before his resignation, Churchill had written to the unit to see if he could find a place. A relatively junior officer, a Captain Kincaid Smith, wrote back to him.

"If you take my advice I should say do anything rather than join a unit within the cavalry corps," he wrote. "You'd be bored to distraction within a week."

HE WAS MET on the dockside in Boulogne by the personal car and driver of Commander in Chief Sir John French who had instructions to take him direct to the British Expeditionary Force (BEF)

HQ at St. Omer.

Churchill persuaded the driver to take him to the QOOH regimental headquarters. A good lunch followed. By early evening, he was with French in his chateau.

The contrast between the luxury of GHQ and the "miserable billets" of the QOOH was striking. Churchill wrote to his wife that he had enjoyed a hot bath, clean bed, "champagne and all the conveniences."

The general was keen for him to take command of a brigade immediately, he said—an appointment that would make him a junior brigadier general commanding more than 5,000 men.

It was exactly what he wanted. Still, Churchill was cautious. First, he said, he wanted to get up to the front line himself to experience conditions.

Churchill told Clementine he was heading to the trenches with the Grenadier Guards. "No action is in prospect and only a very general and ordinary risk need to be contemplated," he wrote. "It is indeed much safer than going into the line with the QOOH."

That last statement was, he knew, a lie.

AGED THIRTY IN November 1915, Clementine—she called herself his "cat"—was almost eleven years his junior. They had been married seven years.

Having met briefly four years earlier, they were first properly introduced at a dinner party in 1908. There was—it seems—an instant attraction (asked years later whether she immediately found him handsome, Clementine diplomatically said she found him "interesting"). A few months later, Churchill wrote to her mother for permission to marry.

Exactly who her father was is far from clear—like both Churchill's own parents, her mother Lady Blanche had a reputation for infidelity. She had grown up in France and Scotland and, when only eighteen, had been secretly engaged to an even older conservative politician, soldier and financier.

By 1915, Clementine and Winston already had three children: Diana, Randolph, and Sarah, the last born while Churchill was haring around Antwerp in 1914. They corresponded frequently.

Clementine's letters would prove vital to keeping Churchill going in the trenches. But the strains and stresses of the war would also push the relationship to its limits.

"I AM EXTREMELY pleased with the way my own affairs have gone—but miserable about the situation in the near East (the Dardanelles)," Churchill wrote on November 17 to his friend Colonel Jack Seely, the only other former Cabinet minister to be serving on the Western Front in uniform. "It is a relief to let all that slide off one's mind and I shall be glad to be back again with the army."

A former Secretary of State for War, Seely—another aristocratic and extremely wealthy Liberal—and Churchill had been friends since the Boer War. Seely, however, had been ousted several months before the war in a dispute over the use of troops to quell a potential uprising in Northern Ireland.

He and Churchill were following parallel

paths. In late 1914, Churchill himself had written privately that Seely—who had just lost his wife as well as his political career—seemed a broken man. Now he was in his element, commanding the Canadian Cavalry Brigade, and something of a legend for leading from the front.

Churchill hoped his own decision to head to the front had begun his own rehabilitation. His papers contain multiple letters from other serving officers expressing their appreciation for his decision.

"I... will not be able to forget how one at least of our masters did not shrink from sharing an existence in Flanders, the likes of which are persistently urged on the people by his colleagues," wrote Royal Flying Corps flight commander Alan Scott. "I have often wondered why so many people write letters to public men. [But] you have stirred my imagination by this effort of yours and it seems natural to write and tell you so."

Another correspondent, Royal Navy Commander Thomas James—executive officer of dreadnaught HMS *Temeraire*—reminded him that it was what he had always wanted.

He recounted a conversation several years earlier aboard Churchill's First Lord of the Admiralty yacht. "[You said] in the event of war with Germany your greatest regret would be that owing to your official position you would be unable to take a fighting part and share in the risks and dangers with the officers of the service," he wrote. "May I say that your fine action is only what one expected of you."

On November 19, Churchill wrote to his brother Jack in the Dardanelles: "I am extremely happy and have regained a peace of mind to which I have long been a stranger."

THE UNIT CHURCHILL was joining, the Grenadier Guards, were the senior and most established infantry regiment in the British Army. The second battalion, which Churchill was joining, was a regular army unit and one of the first sent to France in 1914. It had been there ever since.

As Churchill headed to join them on November 20, the unit was moving up to new positions on the front line around Merville, a village about seventeen miles southeast of St. Omer. By the time he arrived—after yet another lunch with a nearby general—the men were already beginning to move up to their new positions.

According to an account of his time with the Grenadiers, published in 1927,[1] Churchill was found a pony and joined the battalion commander and his staff as they rode forward. It was a dull November afternoon, cold and rainy.

After half an hour of silent progress, the colonel turned to Churchill.

"I think I ought to tell you that we were not at all consulted in the manner of your coming to join us," he said.

Then the adjutant, a captain junior to Churchill who was responsible for much of the battalion's administration, weighed in.

"I'm afraid we have had to cut down on your kit...major," Churchill reported him saying. "We have

---

[1] "At the Front With the Grenadiers" *Nash's – Pall Mall* 78:405 (February 1927)

found a servant for you who is carrying a spare pair of socks and your shaving gear. We have had to leave the rest behind."

Along most of the line, communication trenches ran back from the frontline positions allowing reinforcements and supplies to move back and forth under cover. The lines the Grenadiers were occupying, however—just vacated by Indian army units ill trained for trench combat—had none. That meant the only way in or out of the positions was by moving quickly across the open fields.

"The men have little more than they are standing up in," explained the adjutant.

As they approached the front, the landscape changed. "The shell holes in the neighboring fields became more numerous and the road more broken and littered with debris…the scattered houses changed to ruins. The leafless trees were scarred and split…Night descended and no sound was heard but the crunch of marching feet and the occasional bang of an adjacent gun."

Two miles from the forward trenches, orderlies took control of the horses. From then on, Churchill, the colonel, and the others trudged on foot.

Around half past six, they reached the Grenadiers' new battalion HQ, a half-destroyed collection of buildings, known as Ebenezer Farm. Within an hour or so, they had suffered their first fatality, laid out in the farmyard for burial next day.

The battalion's second-in-command asked Churchill where he wished to sleep. There were two choices: the overcrowded signals room, already occupied by four soldiers, or a nearby dugout.

According to Churchill's account, it took the

battalion's second-in-command and himself more than a quarter of an hour to find the latter. In the darkness and so close to the German lines, they did not dare use torchlight. "It was a sort of pit, four foot deep containing about one foot of water," Churchill wrote. "I thanked the Second in Command for the trouble he had taken in finding its resting place and thought that on the whole I would be better off in the signals office…such was my welcome to the Grenadier Guards."

ACCORDING TO CHURCHILL, the Grenadier commanding officer and his staff "gradually and appreciatively thawed." Churchill asked the colonel if he could accompany him on his morning and evening rounds of the trench positions. "Sometimes when there were a good many bullets he became quite genial," Churchill reported.

For his second night at the front, Churchill suggested he should move forward into one of the frontline trenches with a more junior officer, Captain Edward Gregg. That night, he penned a few hasty words to Clementine.

"Here I am in the line," he wrote. "Except for heavy cannonading—the results of which do not come near us—everything is very quiet…even in the fire trenches of the front line is great tranquility."

Still, he noted, a handful of men were being shot, mainly by stray rounds. He didn't mention the dead Grenadier.

"Any fool can be uncomfortable," an old British Army saying goes. "But a good soldier can make himself comfortable under any condition.

Churchill requested Clementine send him some immediate supplies: a warm brown waistcoat, a pair of trench wading boots, a sleeping bag, two pairs of khaki trousers and a spare pair of boots.

In his 1927 article, Churchill acknowledges another reason for leaving the farm. The Grenadiers—at least in the battalion HQ—practiced a zero tolerance approach to alcohol. "Nothing but strong tea with condensed milk, a very unpleasant beverage, was ever served there," he wrote. "The front line soldiers a few hundred metres forward, however, were offered slightly better flexibility."

The night the battalion moved into the front line, its war diary recorded a heavy frost. Rain was frequent and conditions amongst the worst anywhere on the Western Front. So waterlogged was the soil, Churchill wrote, that conventional trenches and dugouts could barely be built at all.

In a letter to his wife from the rear areas on November 23rd, Churchill outlined the true conditions. The building of trenches and fortifications had fascinated him since Sandhurst. Now he was seriously unimpressed.

"The neglect and idleness of the former tenants is apparent at every step, filth and rubbish everywhere. Graves built into the defences and scattered about promiscuously. Feet and clothing breaking through the soil, water and muck on all sides. And all about this scene in the dazzling moonlight, troops of enormous bats."

He continued: "Amid these surroundings, aided by cold and every minor discomfort, I have found happiness and comfort such as I have not known for many months."

That afternoon, Churchill visited Raymond Asquith, son of the Prime Minister and an officer in another battalion of the Guards. The younger Asquith would be killed later in the year, a loss that would devastate his father.

"Will you send now regularly once a week a *small* box of food to supplement the rations," Churchill wrote, "sardines, chocolate, potted meat and other things which may strike your fancy. Send me also a new pen…I have stupidly lost mine. Send me also lots of love and many kisses."

In a November 24th letter to his mother, Churchill sounds almost like a schoolboy.

"I am very happy here and have made good friends with everybody now. I always get on with soldiers and these are about the best… do you know, I am quite young again?"

From a dugout the following night, he related to Clementine his closest escape of the war so far.

Not long after arriving back in the trenches— and another three-hour move across the exposed and muddy fields—Churchill had received a telegram from the General commanding the corps. The General would like to see him, it said, giving a location some three miles away from which he would be picked up by car.

Grumbling somewhat, Churchill and his soldier servant made their way back across the wasteland, troubled by the occasional passing bullet. On arrival at the road junction, there was no vehicle. There had been an error, a staff officer told him, and the car was unavailable.

Why had the General wanted to see him in the first place? Churchill asked. It was nothing urgent, the staff officer said airily, he just fancied a chat. Another time would do just as well.

Grumbling profusely, Churchill and the soldier began the return journey.

On his return to the forward trenches, they were met by one of the Grenadier sergeants. Churchill's kit had been moved to another dugout, the sergeant said.

"Why?" asked Churchill (according to his 1927 account).

"Yours has been blown up, sir," the senior NCO said, adding that an orderly had been killed. "Better not go in there, sir, it's an awful mess…a whizzbang [high velocity shell] came in through the roof and blew his head off."

In the 1927 account, Churchill says the shell struck five minutes after he left. In the letter to his wife, he says fifteen. Whether he was overstating later for dramatic effect or understating to not alarm Clementine, we shall never know.

On one point both accounts agree, however—he felt much less aggrieved at the General who had got him out of the dugout in the first place.

"Now see from this how vain it is to worry about such things, it is all chance," he wrote to his wife.

THAT NIGHT, CHURCHILL told Clementine he had come across a young soldier who had fallen asleep on sentry duty. "I frightened him dreadfully but did not charge him… he was only a lad and I am not an officer of the regiment. The penalty is death or at least two years."

In signing off, he requested two bottles of brandy and a bottle of peach brandy.

The following day, November 27, the battalion was back in reserve. They had marched out the previous night under bright moonlight, Churchill told Clementine, "singing 'It's a Long Way to Tipperary' while the guns boomed applause."

"It is like getting to a jolly good tavern after a long day's hunting," he continued, "wet and cold and hungry but not without having had sport."

He had been particularly struck by the strict discipline of the battalion, he wrote. There was "a total indifference to death or casualties. What has to be done is done and the losses accepted without fuss or comment." In his time at the front, the 2nd Grenadiers had suffered thirty-five killed and wounded out of a total 700.

BY THE FIRST week of December, Churchill was back in the rear areas, again dining with generals.

He had clearly not been forgotten. On November 30, Lord Curzon—the former Viceroy of India, now in Cabinet as Lord Privy Seal—wrote him a long letter updating him on politics.

On December 3, Churchill himself sent a long memorandum to senior officials on his thoughts on trench warfare in general, particularly his thoughts on a device mounted on caterpillar tracks to push through barbed wire. At the Admiralty, Churchill had been an early proponent of what was to become the tank—still yet to enter service—and he was anxious to be kept up to date.

On December 4, he dined again with Sir John French. According to his letter to Clementine, Churchill said he would be happy with a battalion but French insisted: "a Brigade at once." Anxious to help Churchill see more of the front, the British Expeditionary Force Commander arranged a tour of the French army lines.

On one of his visits to the French sector, Churchill was presented with a French Army helmet: "I am going to wear it as it looks so nice and will perhaps protect my valuable cranium" he told Clementine.

For most of early December, it looked as though Churchill's promotion to Brigadier General was a *fait accompli*. On December 10, he wrote to Clementine asking her to order him a new tunic with the rank.

Having commanded the BEF since 1914 without significant victory, however, French was on the way out. Nothing happened immediately, though, and by December 12 Churchill was back with the Grenadiers waiting to move back to the front.

The good news, he told Clementine, was that his new sleeping bag had arrived and was "divine and glorious... I spent last night in one long purr."

The tins of food from London were now turning up, he said, and his new French Army helmet was the cause of much envy. "I look quite martial in it—like a Cromwellian. I always intend to wear it under fire... but chiefly for appearance."

Back in London, Clementine was seriously worried—and had now clearly seen through the lie that her husband was safer with the Guards than with the cavalry.

"At night when I lie down I say to myself 'thank God he is still alive,' she wrote. "The four weeks of your absence seemed like four years. If only my dear you had no military ambitions. If only you would stay with the Oxfordshire Hussars in their billets."

On December 14, French was withdrawn to London for consultations.

Churchill's letter home the next day mixed high politics and everyday war. In one paragraph, he is relating a raid by some guardsmen on a German trench in which they killed two with clubs and took a third prisoner. In the next, he is pondering whether he should lead a political revolt to bring down Asquith.

In a hastily scribbled postscript later in the day, Churchill recorded he had been phoned directly by French. The Prime Minister had dictated that he should not have a brigade but only a battalion, he said. "You will cancel the order for the tunic!"

Gradually the full picture emerged. Asquith had been nervous of political criticism, particularly from the conservatives, if Churchill was seen to be given at once too high a rank.

Churchill saw this as a personal betrayal. Many of his friends in London, however, had been quietly saying that a battalion command made much more sense as a first step. Had French not been so insistent on a brigade, they said, it would not have been on the table at all.

Although largely unsurprised, Churchill was clearly sorry to see French go. On December 19, the outgoing general made a point of spending most of his last few hours with him.

Churchill's first choice as second-in-command was twenty-nine-year-old Captain Edward Spears, the Francophone liaison officer who had joined him in his tours of the French areas of the front. But Spears was central to Britain's relationship with the French and would be so again in World War II. Much as he wanted to join Churchill, higher powers said he was simply too important to lose.

Churchill turned to Archibald Sinclair, another young protégé he had known before the war. In 1914, Churchill had been involved in attempts to find the young Scottish aristocrat and regular army officer a Liberal constituency to contest as an MP. Now he was staff to Jack Seely with the Canadian cavalry.

Despite their differences in age—Sinclair had just turned twenty-five—they had corresponded frequently. Both were half American, both from families with a colorful reputation for infidelity. Both were fascinated by conflict and politics.

From the start, Sinclair had encouraged Churchill to aim for the command of a "Kitchener battalion," one of the wartime units of volunteers that had swelled the British Army. "No one could object to that on any grounds," he wrote on November 15.

"I [know]…nothing whatever about infantry drill and organisation, but I know a bit about conditions out here, and if I can be any service, and if my general can spare me, you know how proud and eager I would serve you in any capacity."

The new Commander of the British Expeditionary Forces, Sir Douglas Haig, was happy to oblige. "Winston had done good work in the trenches and we were short of Battalion COs," Haig wrote in his diary.

With no battalion immediately available, Churchill was able to return home for Christmas. Clementine had to share his time—he lunched with newspaper editors and Minister for Munitions David Lloyd George, increasingly seen likely to succeed Asquith as Prime Minister.

He returned to France on December 27. Five days later, he was confirmed the new commanding officer of the 6th Battalion, Royal Scots Fusiliers in the 9th (Scottish) Division.

The Fusiliers got no say in the matter.

PETER APPS

Chapter 3 – "An Enormous Bathtub"

When the regimental transport officer first told Captain Andrew Dewar Gibb that Winston Churchill was his new commanding officer, he assumed it was a joke.

"Not to be outdone, I said I knew that…Lord Curzon had, the day before, been made transport officer of the adjoining battalion," he wrote in his memoir.

As Churchill arrived on January 5, the Battalion was in reserve at Moolenacker, some ten miles behind the line.

They already had a commanding officer—Lieutenant-Colonel James Dutton, a Scottish aristocrat who had taken over after his predecessor Herbert Northey was wounded at Loos. He was highly popular and did not want to go.

"As the news spread, a mutinous spirit grew," wrote Gibb. "Everybody liked the old CO and nobody could see why a prominent outsider should come and take its place…Why could not Churchill have gone to the Argylls if he must have a Scottish regiment…?"

Had Churchill replaced a brigadier or more senior officer, he said, there would have been few tears shed. But a battalion—particularly a volunteer battalion such as theirs—was a tightknit family with less than flattering views of those running the war.

The unit, Churchill had already been briefed, was significantly understrength and still recovering from Loos. Many reinforcements had only just arrived and were, in the view of the older hands, barely trained. There was only a single regular officer in the Battalion. All the rest were volunteers.

As eighteen-year-old second lieutenant Jock McDavid watched Churchill and Sinclair arrive, he could not believe his eyes.

The two officers and their two soldier servants arrived in one car, he told the BBC in a 1963 interview. A second car, however, was piled high with luggage "of every description."

"To my amazement, at the very top was a full-length tin bath," he said. "What he was going to do with this I just couldn't think. This…very well-known figure came forward, gave a warm handshake and introduced himself as Lieutenant-Colonel Winston Churchill."

THE IMPRESSION DID not immediately improve. According to nineteen-year-old Edmund Hakewill-Smith—the only regular officer and a future general—Churchill's initial welcoming speech was terrible.

"Gentlemen, I am now your commanding officer," he said. "Those who support me I will look after. Those who go against me, I will break. Good afternoon, gentlemen."

"Everyone was agreed we were in for a pretty rotten time," he later told Churchill's official biographer Gilbert.

Later that afternoon, Churchill called together all the battalion officers and senior NCOs in his headquarters, a farmhouse Gibb describes as "more than usually dirty".

The farm's original occupants were still there. Through means of sign language, they had apparently been told the new colonel was, somehow, "somebody."

As each company commander was introduced to Churchill, Gibb says the former First Lord sat back in his chair to scrutinize them, "silently and intently, from head to foot." It was a process Gibb said appeared to be designed to help remember their names.

Gibb judged it "distasteful." He was later to try it himself to memorize the names of his platoon sergeants. "I think it upset me more than it did them and I never did learn their names," he complained.

OVERNIGHT, THE BATTALION headquarters was a hive of activity. According to Gibb, by the following morning a visible change was apparent.

An "ancient and far from sober looking" military policeman had been replaced with a "smart, tall soldier with a great deal of equipment." The regimental sergeant major—with or without prompting—had tidied himself until his buttons shone. After further sign language with the French occupants of the farm, agricultural activity had largely ceased.

There was even, according to Gibb, "a slight sympathetic smartening of the clothing worn by the officers."

"War is declared, gentlemen, on the lice," announced Churchill theatrically before launching into an apparently spectacular speech on the tiny insects, their life cycle and their imminent destruction.

For three or four days, the entire farm was

taken up with several hundred men taking hot steam irons to every item of clothing. Giant brewery vats were brought in for almost everything to be boiled. "We were certainly a liceless Battalion," wrote Gibb.

GIVEN HOW CLOSE they ultimately became, it is striking how commander and subordinates initially failed to "get" each other.

It is not, perhaps, entirely Churchill's fault. In his briefings, he had been warned to expect a unit grossly ill prepared for front-line duties.

"There is not a single regular officer in the regiment, the senior officers have all been shot in the battle," he wrote to Clementine the day before his arrival. "Only quite young boys remain…it will be an exhausting labour but I expect I shall succeed."

The day of his arrival, he wrote that he was now "up to my neck in very small things."

On the evening of January 6—the day of his "lice" speech—he wrote another letter which started even more negatively.

"This regiment is pathetic. The young officers are also small middle-class Scotsmen—brave and willing and intelligent but of course all quite new to soldiering. All the seniors and professionals have fallen."

Then, in the next sentence, there is a jarring change of tone to the positive.

"I spent the morning watching each company to drill and handle their stop they are very good. The mess is also well-managed—much better than that of the Grenadiers. The regiment is full of life…I believe I shall be a help to them. Archie [Sinclair] is very happy and I hope he will be made a major."

"This is a disorganised sort of letter but you must make allowances! My strong natural vitality and carry me along."

Despite being only twenty-five, Sinclair—who, despite Churchill's lobbying, remained a captain for the time being—clearly was a pillar of strength. Without him, it's doubtful Churchill or the battalion would have performed so well. He had his own experience of frontline warfare with Jack Seely's Canadians. But, as he had himself pointed out in his November letter to Churchill, the career cavalry officer also had no genuine experience himself at all of a line infantry regiment.

In his description of the battalion in *With Churchill at the Front*, Gibb describes what could almost be a different unit. For sure, it had little in the way of regular officers. But a volunteer "Kitchener battalion" was always going to have a very different spirit and style to a regular or even territorial unit.

Gibb himself was twenty-eight, three years older than Sinclair. He might have lacked Sinclair's aristocratic and political pedigree but he more life experience, a university education from Glasgow University, and a time practicing law.

Exactly when he had joined the battalion is not entirely clear—there is certainly no suggestion that it was one of the survivors of Loos. But he had clearly spent some time in the line.

Clearly, those who had been at Loos had been traumatized by the experience. It had been the first heavy pitched battle fought by the volunteer "new armies." Losses were so heavy that the man tasked with taking over the Battalion afterwards—the then

Major Dutton—admitted in his official report that it was hard to reconstruct what had happened.

Lieutenant Colonel Northey's personal journal was—unusually—included in the official Battalion War Diary. He described scenes of chaos, carnage, and trenches choked with dead.

According to the War Diary—a scrappy, almost invariably handwritten record now by the UK National Archives—the remnants of the unit moved almost immediately to the Ypres Salient. They remained rotating in and out of the front line there for the rest of the year, finishing on December 18. Two phrases stand out repeatedly in several different hands: "very heavy shelling" and "very, very wet."

New reinforcements—including most of the officers—were arriving. By Gibb's judgment, the Battalion was by early 1916 "in a fair way to become again as fine a unit as it was in the spring of 1915."

THE MEN WERE largely lowland Scots with occasional northern English. Some were farmers, some miners, some industrial workers. The initial volunteers had signed up *en masse* at the outbreak. By early 1916, those that survived knew their jobs well and had few illusions on the realities of warfare.

Then, as now, the most basic unit of the battalion was the infantry section, a ten-man team of soldiers each led by a corporal. While many of the private soldiers were new, the corporals would have been rather more experienced. Many had been in since the beginning.

Four sections comprised a platoon under a junior officer with a sergeant as his deputy.

Eighteen-year-old Jock MacDavid had certainly been there in November and December in Sanctuary Wood near Ypres, though. His signature appears clearly in the War Diary for that period.

In his account, Gibb—like many junior officers of the time —makes it clear that he viewed more senior officers (including initially Churchill) as primarily irritants. At best, they were entertaining. At worst, they were dangerous.

Gibb's account was initially published anonymously under the pseudonym "Captain X," though he eventually accepted credit for it. He refers to himself in the third person throughout—often as "the unhappy Gibb." But he provides the only truly full account of the battalion and its personalities.

At the time Churchill took over, A Company was commanded by a captain named Foulkes ("most deplorable of horsemen and most lovable of men," according to Gibb). Gibb himself commanded B Company, Harvey ("handsome and impressive") C Company. D Company was under a Captain Ramsay, a "gallant and efficient officer who possessed in the highest degree that quality, more desirable than any other in the late war, an ever present appreciation of such humour as lay in the most humourless situations." All now found themselves with new routines.

None of them knew what to make of Churchill. "Our nights were spent wondering what he would do next, our days in doing it," wrote Gibb.

ON THE MORNING of January 7, the entire battalion was instructed to parade in a nearby meadow. There was much grumbling.

Churchill was still finding his feet, hugely dependent on Sinclair. "Archie does a vast amount of household work," he wrote to Clementine. "The young officers are also made to do their full share."

Churchill told Clementine this was the first time the entire battalion had paraded *en masse* rather than in separate companies. He was "anxious to make them feel that corporate identity and a sense of my own control. A colonel within his own sphere is an autocrat who punishes and promotes and displaces at his discretion."

The saving grace, Gibb and the officers hoped, was that as cavalrymen neither Churchill nor Sinclair would notice if their infantry drills were wrong.

Churchill went along the lines of Fusiliers company by company and platoon by platoon, talking to every soldier.

"He was very nice to them and I have to say they responded well," wrote Gibb. In going down the lines, he felt Churchill—either by accident or design—had overlooked multiple under-shined buttons and deficiencies other officers would have commented on.

Next, Churchill ordered Gibb's company to practice bayonet drill. The company's senior noncommissioned officer had just begun barking out orders when Churchill came back over.

"No, no, I want you to do it," Churchill said. Nor was he content with letting Gibb simply lecture. He insisted the (now definitely "unhappy" captain) actually demonstrate it himself.

The only regular, Sandhurst-qualified

Hakewell-Smith, was unimpressed. Most of Churchill's drill commands were wrong, he later told biographer Gilbert.

That night, orders were posted for the battalion to parade again the following day. This time, the company commanders were to be mounted on horseback.

CHURCHILL SEEMS TO have avoided referencing the following day's parade.

According to Gibb, it began with promise. Appearances were notably improved. Somewhat to his own surprise, he got himself onto the company horse, "Eagle," who, he said, resembled a "giant trench rat."

The other companies were rather more confused, he claims. D Company had not turned up at all.

Eventually, it arrived "with piper playing...Ramsey looking happy and well fed." Churchill let it pass (although only for the moment— Ramsey was later pulled to one side, moved from his company and given a different role).

It was chaos. Foulkes lost control of his horse, his company almost marched into a hedge and the entire parade came close to breaking up.

Churchill seems to have spent the rest of the day at brigade headquarters. With the brigade commander apparently off sick, he found himself temporarily—and apparently largely theoretically—in command of the entire formation including several other battalions. By the evening the brigadier had returned and he was back with the Fusiliers.

The relationship was straining both Churchill and his subordinates.

"I tried to make the arrangements and give them all the feeling that there is something behind them and that they are strongly commanded," Churchill wrote to Clementine on January 10, adding that he found himself privately "feeling deeply the injustice" of his removal from power.

"I do not ever show anything but a smiling face to the military world," he continued. "But so it is a relief to pour one's heart out to you. Bear with me."

CHURCHILL'S ATTEMPTS TO get his officers on horseback was not as anachronistic as it sounds. With the desperately muddy conditions of the Western front, the only primitive motor vehicles in service were restricted to a handful of paved roads—roads which were increasingly crumbling under heavy use and artillery fire.

The age of the cavalry might have almost been over—although Jack Seely would lead the Canadians in the last great cavalry charge of the war as late as 1918—but horses were vital. Most units kept dozens if not more, both to haul equipment, guns, and ammunition. Often, it was still the fastest and easiest way of transport across significant distances.

Seely was not the only senior officer to keep his personal mount near him at all times. Douglas Haig spent many of his days too on horseback. The new tranche of volunteer officers, many from the urban middle classes, however, came from very different backgrounds.

The prospect that some of his officers might be simply unable to ride, Gibb concluded, had simply not occurred to Churchill.

But towards the most forward trenches, walking or crawling would be the order of the day. And Churchill was determined his battalion would be up to speed on those techniques as well.

Nineteen-year-old Hakewill-Smith was put to work instructing the men in grenades. Accidents were frequent, Churchill told his wife, with several Fusiliers inadvertently dropping the devices instead of throwing them. "Then the bombing officer…deftly picked it up and throws it away with perhaps a second to spare over," he wrote. "Everyone has to learn. It is perfectly safe as long as you do it right."

Soon Hakewill-Smith had his nickname: "bomb boy."

The Christmas hamper Clementine had ordered from Fortnum and Mason finally arrived January 10. But the tinned goods in it, he told her, would be kept for the trenches.

A few days later, he tracked down a piano and organized a party and "sports day," a rambunctious affair including pillow fights and obstacle races. "The men enjoyed themselves immensely," he told Clementine on January 17. "Poor fellows, nothing like this had ever been done for them before they do not get much brightness in their lives, short though they may be."

"The Battalion is the weakest of the brigade and makes the least good appearance," he had written the previous day, noting that both the brigade divisional commanders were aware of the difficulties and largely leaving him to solve them.

By January 18, he was more enthusiastic—perhaps the concert and sports helped. "I think they are coming well into hand," he told Clementine. But he complained of an increasingly "distinctly hostile tone" from the staff officers at brigade headquarters.

"I have a horrible suspicion that the brigadier—who is not a success as I told you—thinks I have been put here to supersede him after a brief interval—or else his staff do," he confided, adding: "Archie thinks this may be the case because their attitude is quite unusual."

For the whole war, Churchill had been underwhelmed by the commanders and horrified by the deadlock on the Western front. The state of modern military technology, he believed, favored the defender and made attacks costly and all but impossible.

He attended a lecture for mid- and senior-ranking officers on the Battle of Loos. The final estimate of casualties, he told Clementine, within the Scottish Ninth Division alone was 6,000 killed and wounded out of a total 10,000.

"Afterwards, they asked what was the lesson of the lecture," he wrote. "I restrained the impulse to reply: 'Don't do it again.' But they will, I have no doubt."

Still, he said, the good news was that he was finally getting his biweekly bath.

Back in London, Clementine was feeling the strain. In her January 16 letter, she begged Churchill to get forty-eight hours leave to meet her in the French port Dieppe. "I do so long to see you," she wrote. "I am very, very lonely."

There was no leave to be had. They were

heading into the line.

PETER APPS

Chapter 4 – "Plugstreet"

Of all the areas along the Western Front, the Ypres Salient was by far the least loved by the British Army. They had been fighting to protect it since 1914 and were thoroughly sick of it.

"Who discovered the Salient?" asked satirical British trench newspaper the *Wipers Times* in its second ever edition on February 28 under "Things We Want to Know." "Why?"

A "salient" was not itself a true geographical feature—the ground there was scarcely higher than elsewhere. Instead, it referred to an area of ground held by one side protruding into enemy territory and therefore surrounded on three sides.

After the near collapse of Belgium at the outbreak of war, the area around Ypres was almost the only part of the country still in Allied hands. Keeping it that way was a top Allied priority.

In 1916, the sector was between major campaigns. The second Battle of Ypres had concluded in May of 1915 and the third—more commonly known as Passchendaele—would not begin until April 1917. It would see yet another two further pitched battles by the end of the war.

For most of the year, the real strategic focus was simply elsewhere. At the end of February, the German army would launch its major offensive against Verdun, the start of an onslaught that would last the rest of the year and become perhaps the largest action in human history with more than a million men on either side.

For the British, the main effort was already switching to Somme in France where in July the BEF would launch its largest, most disastrous attack of the war.

Along the rest of the front, the priority was simply holding the line, keeping enough pressure on the Germans to limit the volume of resources they could throw against Verdun.

"It was a heavy duty—weary months of desultory trench fighting with no combined movement, no great offensive purpose with spirit," wrote novelist John Buchan in his history of the Royal Scots Fusiliers regarding the first half of 1916. "It was costly duty for the average daily loss was 500 (along the entire front held by the BEF) which gives in six months a total of 90,000 men."

The trenches stretched more than 500 miles from the North Sea to Switzerland. Against most of the front, sectors would go through both quiet and noisy spells. Ypres, however, was always under fire.

ON JANUARY 20, with the Fusiliers still training, Churchill made his first trip to the frontline sector around "Plugstreet" where the battalion was to be deployed. Last time he had been there, he had been a minister. Now learning the terrain would be a matter of life and death.

The previous day, he had recounted to Clementine how the brigade commander had praised the improvement in his men. He was still worried about relations with the brigade staff—particularly a major who he felt might have had his own hopes of taking over the battalion had Churchill not come— but felt he was gradually winning them over.

Churchill's January 21st letter finished with a

request that Clementine send him out a typewriter. "I want to instill more order and style into my official correspondence," he wrote, clearly thinking of his letters to Lloyd George, Asquith and others. "At present we scribble in pencil and it all seems very slipshod."

ON JANUARY 23, the day before the battalion moved up, Churchill found time to write to his five-year-old son Randolph. "I am living here in a little farm," he wrote. "It is not so pretty as Hoe Farm [where the Churchills spent summer 1915] and there are no nice flowers and a pond or trees... but there are three large fat dirty pigs. Like the ones we saw in the wood."

Then the tone darkens. "The Germans are a long way off and cannot shoot at us here," he reassured his son, adding, though, that the sounds of artillery could be heard all night. "Soon we are going to go close after the Germans and then we shall shoot back at them and try to kill them. This is because they have done wrong and caused all this war and sorrow...write me a letter yourself soon and I will send you another back."

Morale, Gibb wrote, was mixed at best. The battalion was seriously understrength. According to Churchill, they were moving into the line with some 700 men, 200 less than the battalion they were replacing. On paper, they should have had more than 1000.

Churchill organized one last, spectacular dinner party at a nearby hotel. There was champagne and oysters.

"I wish I could write of the dinner party as it merits to be written of," writes Gibb. "But only salient features remain in my memory—no bad test of its success."

Churchill, he said, made an eloquent speech, saying amongst other things that he had found in Scotland the three best things in his life: "My wife, my constituency, and my regiment." The battalion piper played, copious amounts were drunk.

Around 11 p.m. the party broke up and they rode—or walked—drunkenly back to the farm buildings. Some of the officers and men disappeared into the nightspots of the nearby town. The doctor and transport officer, Gibb claims, did not return until the morning.

ON A COLD raw day in January, Gibb, Churchill and a detachment of officers and fusiliers boarded a London motor omnibus that wended its way through the battered filthy towns of northern France. It dropped them in the town of Amentieres. From there, they were expected to walk to Ploegsteert for a final handover of the positions they were to occupy.

It was here that Churchill made his somewhat offbeat comment about being "recalled from the Senate" to the battlefields of France and one of the 8th Border regiment recognized—or almost recognized—that the man in the French helmet was actually Winston Churchill.

Many biographers attribute Churchill's use of his French helmet to his never-ending desire to be noticed. Gibb, however, felt the opposite was true.

Without the French helmet, he says, the young Scottish soldier who stopped him would unquestionably have recognized Churchill. As it was, Gibb was able to pass the encounter off by saying the resemblance "had often been remarked on." The soldier moved on, he wrote, apparently satisfied he had been mistaken.

Churchill himself worked to avoid leaving too many clues as to where he was. His name never appears once in the battalion war diary—all the entries were written and signed by subordinates such as Sinclair and Gibb.

Even with all the shells they would receive, Churchill maintained there would be more if the Germans knew he was there.

"I am just as well known in Germany as [German Admiral] Tirpitz is in England and they don't like me there," Gibb relates him saying. "They hate me. If they knew I was in the front line here they wouldn't send just a few shells…They would turn on all their guns and blot the place out."

McDavid was later to recall a similar comment. "If they thought I was here they would have obliterated the countryside for twenty miles around," he quoted Churchill as saying.

It was evening before the guides were finished showing the officers everything they needed to see. Another omnibus took them back to the battalion.

Such privileged access to vehicles, Gibb grumbled in his book almost a decade later, was distinctly unusual for Scottish troops. More often than their English counterparts, he felt, the Scots were left to walk.

CHURCHILL AND GIBB are somewhat contradictory in their dating of events in January. It is not entirely clear whether Churchill made one or more trips to Ploegsteert. But he was clearly not unhappy with the location.

"It is much the best bit of line I have seen all along the front," he wrote. "It is dry—the trenches are boarded and drained. The wire is good. The field of fire is clear. I think we could stand a pretty good pounding here with comparatively little loss."

On the morning of January 24, one of the battalion's officers—the handwriting suggests it was Archie Sinclair—began a new page in the battalion's war diary. "Marched off from billets at 8am," he wrote.

According to Gibb there was "the usual cursing and grousing," but it was a warmer, more pleasant day. The war diary records that within three and a half hours they reached the village of Lacreche and halted overnight. At six o'clock the following morning, they moved off for Ploegsteert, arriving just over two hours later.

The battalion HQ—including Churchill—settled into some convent buildings in the center of the village. Several nuns were still in residence and were soon co-opted—" seduced," in Churchill's words—into providing cooked food for the occupants. The other companies, meanwhile, bedded down in outlying farms.

Around 4 a.m., Gibb says he and Ramsay were awakened by a runner from battalion HQ. Gibb reached around for a match by which to read the message. Soon, he was heartily cursing Churchill.

According to the message, the CO wished his company commanders to be aware that the wind and other conditions were perfect for a German gas attack. What they should do with this information, it did not say. The clear suggestion was that they should wake their men and tell them the same.

"Good God", said Ramsay. "The man's daft."

"Daft or not daft, I'm hanged if I'm going out at this time of night on any such quest," Gibb replied and told the orderly to go away.

There was no gas.

PARTICULARLY WITH HIS reputation after the Dardanelles, Churchill was at pains to reassure his men he would take no unnecessary risks.

"We will go easy at first, a little digging and feeling our way," Gibb reported him saying. "And then, perhaps later on, we may attempt a deed."

Throughout the war, senior British commanders had been worried that the often static conditions of trench warfare might undermine the army's "offensive spirit."

For those in the line, it was almost a bad joke. "Are we offensive enough?" asked the strapline of the *Wipers Times*, mocking the repeated edicts from GHQ.

Along quieter stretches of the front, there were reports of a "live and let live" attitude. In such locations, German and Allied forces appeared to reach an informal, usually unspoken agreement whereby they avoided too much activity against each other to keep casualties down for both sides.

Such approaches were rarer around Ypres—

the level of fighting and artillery fire was usually simply too intense to allow such feelings to develop. Still, "Plugstreet" had been the site of the famous Christmas 1914 truce in which British and German soldiers had emerged from the trenches and played football in no man's land.

"Deeds," Gibb complains, had therefore become "unpleasantly popular." Troops on the front line were encouraged to mount raids on nearby trenches, patrols to dominate no man's land.

Such moves were deeply unpopular. "The ordinary mental state of mind slogging to and from trench was miles and miles from the heroic," wrote Gibb.

BOTH CHURCHILL AND Gibb were seriously struck by the resilience of the Belgian civilians still living in the village. Several times, Churchill mentioned in his letters that there were women and children living within a few hundred meters of their reserve positions.

The village, he discovered, had been briefly occupied by the Germans for a week in 1914 before British troops had driven them back.

There was little time to settle in. Having arrived on January 25, the Fusiliers were to move into the line barely twenty-four hours later.

Churchill penned yet another letter to Clementine. Not as many would come in the following weeks, he said, although they would remain one of his highest priorities.

"My daily letter to you makes inroads into my time equal to the pleasure and relief it gives me to write," he said. "I had almost lost the art of writing…I am gradually regaining it through my missives to you, my darling one…"

The afternoon before moving up, Churchill called together his officers. According to Gibb, he warned them the following day would be the Kaiser's birthday and they might expect heavy shelling from the very start.

To Clementine the following day, Churchill recounted his advice.

"Don't be careless about yourselves—on the other hand not too careful," he said. "Keep a special pair of boots to sleep in and only get them wet in a real emergency. Use alcohol in moderation but don't have a great parade of bottles in your dugout. Live well but don't flaunt it."

Some of the more junior officers, Churchill knew, were now heading into danger for the first time. They were amongst those who would face the greatest risk and on whom he would be most dependent on hold the unit together.

"Laugh a little, and teach your men to laugh— great good humour under fire. War is a game that is played with a smile. If you can't smile, grin. If you can't grin, stay out of the way till you can."

It was clearly a presentation Churchill was proud of. In his letter to Clementine, he rather spoils the effect by saying so.

"Since Polonius advice to Laertes there had been nothing like it," he said, referring to a speech in Shakespeare's *Hamlet*.

By the time biographer Gilbert questioned McDavid in the 1960s, Churchill had substantially raised the bar for inspiring, reassuring speeches. But this one, the former subaltern believed, still stood the test of time. "It was a good pep talk," he told him.

IT WAS A fine moonlit night as the Fusiliers made their way forward. It was also, according to Gibb, "shockingly early"—around 2 a.m.—and all ranks in the Battalion grumbled, happily blaming their new commander.

By all accounts, the procedure itself went remarkably smoothly. According to the War Diary, by 5:30 a.m. the Fusiliers were in position and the previous unit—the 2nd Battalion, South Lancashire Regiment—was making its way back to Ploegsteert.

Almost immediately, Gibb says, the German artillery opened up.

To read Churchill or even Gibb on shelling can make it feel like little more than an irritation. But the howitzer, not the machine gun, was the deadliest weapon of the conflict. And the casualties—both the aggregate numbers and the individual injuries—could be horrific.

The German 77 mm shell—the most used on the Western front—was designed to shatter into 500 splinters, each one potentially lethal. Roughly 59 percent of all British wounds came from shellfire compared to about 39 percent from gunshots. And the wounds were often much worse. In the French army, men were three times more likely to die from shell wounds than that from a rifle.[2]

Who lived and died, Churchill had already discovered with the Grenadiers, was arbitrary and

[2] Gary Sheffield, *Forgotten Victory,* Kindle location 2123

unfair.

"If anyone will look back over the course of even 10 years' experience, you will see what tiny incidents, unimportant in themselves, have in fact governed the whole of his fortunes and career," he would write in 1927. "This is true of ordinary life. But in war, which is an intense form of life, Chance casts aside all veils and disguises and presents herself nakedly from moment to moment as the direct arbiter of all persons and events.

"Starting out in the morning you leave your matches behind you. Before you have gone 100 yards, you return to get them and thus miss the shell which arrived for your express benefit from 10 miles away…You walk to the right or the left of a particular tree and it makes the difference whether you rise to command an Army Corps or are sent home crippled or paralysed for life."

In this case, nerves were frayed but casualties avoided. By the time Churchill reached the positions now occupied by Gibb and his men, soldiers were already beginning to patch damaged parapets.

Churchill told them to stop.

"Let them remain as they are till dark," he told Gibb. "Don't let them see that we are hit or that it is anything material."

It was, Gibb decided, a reasonable decision. But after one of his men was quickly shot and wounded through a hole in the trench parapet, however, he had his men make repairs anyway.

Whether Churchill ever noticed is not recorded. He was ferociously busy. According to his letter to Clementine that evening, he spent three hours in the trenches that morning visiting each rifle company and providing advice on defensive positions.

As he wrote, Sinclair was making his own rounds. Churchill would again visit every position in the battalion himself later that night, he said. "It takes nearly two hours to traverse this labyrinth of mud," he told her.

CONDITIONS IN THE battalion HQ at Laurence Farm were marginally better—and certainly drier—than in the forward positions. But privations were rife. Cooking was often difficult or impossible by day when the smoke from a fire might attract shells or snipers.

Churchill was determined to make as good a life of it as possible. Clementine, he said, should send him as much tinned food as she could: "big slabs of corned beef, stilton cheeses, cream, hams, sardines, dried fruits." A big beefsteak pie might also work, he said, although nothing too rich such as grouse. "The simpler the better and substantial too, for our ration meat is tough and tasteless…"

THE BASIC SETUP for the sixth Royal Scots Fusiliers at "Plugstreet" would be broadly similar to that of the Grenadiers. As then, they would rotate between the frontline trenches and a rear reserve position in the town, alternating throughout with another unit. When they were in the line, most of the company—including the platoon and company commanders—would be in the foremost trenches of the firing line. Churchill's battalion headquarters would be 500 meters further back, connected to the front line positions by telephone.

The building Churchill was taking over as his headquarters—"Lawrence Farm", although its original French name was almost certainly different—had already been struck eight or ten times by shells, he told Clementine. He was, he told her "rather tempted" to move instead to the subterranean cellars of a nearby convent. For the time being, however, they were flooded and would require a great deal of preparation.

Most of Churchill's heavier kit—including, it seems, the bathtub—were to be kept in the battalion's reserve positions in the village roughly another kilometer away. That, Churchill wrote, would be convenient. But it would also mean that the battalion would be within German artillery range the entire time.

As he had hoped, it was not the worst place on the front. Churchill told Clementine he had been talking to one of the private soldiers from the Borders regiment they were relieving. "I asked…whether he was not very glad that after three months in the firing line to be getting some rest," he wrote. "He replied that he was rather sorry as they would never get such a good place again."

On January 27, Archie Sinclair recorded the battalion's first fatality, a soldier killed near one of the farms Lancashire soldiers had used as a support base.

"Up at 3 AM after a disturbed night, orders coming in etc as all day," Churchill told Clementine. "I am sleepy. But I shall have another broken night tonight"

January 28, Sinclair wrote, was a fine day with

less shelling but considerable aerial activity over the battlefield. Snipers, however, were very active and another soldier was wounded.

By midnight the next day, the unit that would alternate in and out of the trenches with the Fusiliers throughout Churchill's time in the trenches were making their way up from "Plugstreet."

By 6:25 a.m., the Battalion was back in their reserve positions. Which, Sinclair recorded neatly in the War Diary, was then shelled with high explosive shells.

BACK IN LONDON at their family home of 41 Cromwell Road, Clementine's responsibilities went well beyond finding Churchill tinned food—although he was most assiduous in reminding her to make sure she billed him for any such purchases.

Out of immediate touch himself with the political elite, she was Churchill's ambassador. She hosted dinners, took cabinet ministers and newspaper editors to lunch, dined with Asquith and his family in Downing Street. At the same time, she was opening a string of canteens for munition workers.

In his letters, Churchill demanded regular press cuttings and updates on all the matters of the day. In particular, he was interested in the gradual rise of David Lloyd George amid the political battles over conscription. Those two trends, he believed, offered his best hope for return.

He was often repetitive. He was continuously mulling in his letters to her over what jobs he might take in government—perhaps a newly formed Air Ministry—and under what terms. Clearly, he missed being in government terribly. Many of his letters were dominated by expressions of bitterness and envy to those he felt had betrayed him.

"Well, this is a moody letter," he had written on January 19. "Six o'clock is a bad hour for me. I feel the need of power as an outlet worst then and the energy of body and mind is strong within me."

Clementine was more concerned for his life. But she was convinced he was doing the right thing, both for himself and his future career.

"My darling, through all your moods, never regret resigning at the moment you did," she wrote on January 20 in a letter that must have arrived just as he reached the front. "You would have been terribly miserable doing nothing in England."

Still, she said, she was deeply worried that his battalion was so weak. She entreated him desperately to always wear his helmet, pushed him to move its headquarters to a potentially more secure cellars nearby.

Her letter of January 30 was particularly alarmed. The newspapers in London were full of talk of a German offensive and she had not heard from him for six days. She did not know where he was.

Churchill's letters were less censored than most from the frontline—indeed, either he or Sinclair would often mark them with the official censor stamp themselves to avoid others reading them. But he had still not told her exactly where they were.

Clementine had not known Churchill in his war reporter days. She must have assumed that—Zeppelin air raids on London aside—he would have a largely safe war. Now there was nothing particularly special or unusual about the fears she faced every day.

And she knew it.

"I hope you love me very much darling," she concluded her January 20 letter. "I long for you often. I wake up in the night and think of you in your squalid billet and of all the women in Europe who are lying awake praying for the safety of their men."

Chapter 5 – Shelling and Snow

The world Churchill now inhabited was shared with millions of soldiers of all sides. Their experiences would define a generation and shape the rest of the century.

"Before the war it had seemed incredible that such terrors and slaughters, even if they began, could last more than a few months," Churchill would write in 1927. "After the first two years it was difficult to believe that they would ever end."

As the Fusiliers settled into Ploegsteert, a twenty-six-year-old Adolf Hitler was serving as a runner on the Somme. In the skies overhead, Herman Goering flew with Manfred von Richtofen, the legendary "Red Baron." Future French leader Charles de Gaulle would shortly arrive at Verdun commanding a company. And in the trenches of the Eastern front, Russian troops were on the brink of mutiny that would fuel a revolution.

In their early years in the Army, Churchill and his contemporaries had lamented that the age of great European wars had been over more than a century. "Fancy being 19 in 1793 with more than 20 years of war against Napoleon in front of one," he would later recall thinking. "What splendour we should have had."

The reality, he wrote home, was wretched.

"The same conditions and features reproduce themselves in every section," Churchill told Clementine on March 17. "Shattered buildings, sandbag habitations, trenches heavily wired, shell holes, frequent graveyards with thickets of little crosses, wild rank growing grass, muddy roads, khaki soldiers—and so on for hundreds and hundreds of miles…Miserable Europe."

Their initial spell in the front line had been only forty-eight hours. Thereafter, the Fusiliers would spend six days in and six out. It was a broadly typical pattern—the average British soldier would spend perhaps 100 days a year in the trenches, the rest in training or reserve. The reserve positions at "Plugstreet," however, were so close to the front that they too would be under near perpetual shellfire.

In his letters home, Churchill did his best to reassure Clementine. The German gunners were predominantly targeting British artillery pieces nearby, he said, and so the town itself was struck relatively little. As the days and weeks progressed, however, that line became ever less tenable.

Some shells were already coming too close for comfort. One landed particularly close by the convent just after he had emerged from his bath, he told his mother in a letter, sending soot cascading down the chimney into his room and all over him.

"I am increasingly fatalistic in my moods…and do not worry at all at the dangers when they come," he told her. Only the greater picture of the war—and his inability to affect it—continued to depress him. "I only fret when I think of the many things that ought to be done and my real powers are unused at this great time."

Still, he remained the leading celebrity on his sector of the front and there were no shortage of visitors willing to brave the danger to see him.

His first senior visitor was F.E. Smith, a longtime political ally, then Attorney General and one of his few true close friends. He was to dine in at

Churchill's rear headquarters in the village on January 29. He had brought with him the new typewriter and an assortment of tinned goods from Clementine. (Smith would be one of many senior officials shanghaied into acting as his personal courier.)

But Smith did not arrive. It transpired he had been arrested in the rear area for not having the correct pass.

Churchill, Hakewill-Smith later reported, was furious. A car was summoned.

As it happened, Minister for Munitions David Lloyd George and Home Secretary Bonar Law were also visiting France. Churchill met with them and they ultimately found Smith at a nearby Canadian headquarters. (By this time, he had simply walked out of military detention.)

The Canadian headquarters was home to another who was to become one of Churchill's closest and most controversial cronies, Max Aitken—the future Lord Beaverbrook. Never trusted by Clementine and always rumored to be corrupt, Beaverbrook would take control of Britain's aircraft industry in 1940 and play a crucial role in winning the Battle of Britain.

The Smith incident sparked a furious round of letters and official communications. Initially, at least, Churchill seems to have taken the whole matter extremely seriously.

"I still have not been able to make out what exactly happened," he wrote to Clementine on February 1. Some relatively junior military authorities, he thought, had been trying to make a point, and it had all got out of hand. "Of course he should have had proper papers," he noted in brackets.

According to Gilbert's official biography of Churchill, Smith was the victim of a practical joke. An order instructing units in the area to find him and issue him a pass if he did not have one had been amended to instead have him arrested.

By then, however, Churchill had other concerns. The Fusiliers were back in the lines.

THE FIRST GERMAN barrage—although that term would not come into popular usage until later in the war—struck shortly after their arrival. According to Churchill, four men were wounded, several seriously. The battalion doctor was not immediately available and the wounded received inadequate attention, he noted angrily.

The Fusiliers got through several medical officers in Churchill's time, Gibb wrote. This one did not last.

Churchill persuaded the British guns to lay down an even heavier retaliation, he told Clementine, "and we gave them a good deal more than we received. But of course one cannot tell what results were produced."

"Darling—do you like me to write these things to you?" he asked. "They are the ordinary incidents of life here—they are dangerous but not very dangerous...I would not write to you about them if I though the account would cause you extra anxiety. But I think you like to know the dimensions of the dangers and what they are like."

He had spent most of the day in the forward trenches, he said. He also had to be inoculated against tetanus after injuring himself while showing how "easy" it was to cut barbed wire.

Such activity, Gibb writes, was entirely typical, particularly in the early days. "Winston certainly got some work out of his battalion," he wrote. "Early and late he was in the line. On average he went round three times a day which was no mean task in itself as he had plenty of other work to do. At least one of these visits was after dark, usually about 1am."

Churchill was, he says, a striking and distinctive sight. In wet weather—near continuous for much of this period—he would storm through the trenches in a waterproof jacket, trousers and knee-high waders. Even after the rest of the battalion was issued steel helmets, he kept wearing his French tin hat.

"He was always in the closest touch with every piece of work that was going on," says Gibb. "And while at times his demands were a little extravagant, his kindliness and the humour that never failed to flash out made everybody only too keen to get on with the work, whether the ideal he pointed out to them was unattainable or not."

He would expound volubly on the correct way of setting up sandbags, Gibb continues. "You felt sure from his grasp of practice that he must have served apprentice to a bricklayer and a master mason."

Between the wars, Churchill would develop a serious taste for bricklaying, building his own cottage at his country house in Chartwell and even joining the bricklayers trade union. But the reality in the trenches, Gibb said, was that sometimes he was simply wrong.

According to Gibb, he also had the annoying

habit of repeatedly comparing the work of his soldiers to the battalion they alternated with, the Gordon Highlanders. As a rule, most battalions loved to complain about the others they shared the trenches with. Churchill, however, seemed to hold up the Highlanders' work as superior to the Fusiliers.

Relations between the two regiments were already less than rosy and Churchill's fulsome praise for them made it no better. "We had already heard so much of the Gordons' achievements, both from their own lips and from the daily papers that to have them hurled at our head by the CO…was a little too much."

LAWRENCE FARM WAS hit for the first time on February 3, a day after Churchill had told Clementine they had had a period of "profound peace…not a shell…hardly a bullet."

It was another high velocity shell—a "whizz-bang"—the same type that had wrecked Churchill's bunker with the Grenadiers in December.

According to an account McDavid later gave Churchill's biographer Gilbert, the entire battalion HQ staff had a very lucky escape. (Gibb says they were almost "blotted out.")

According to Churchill's own letter home, he and his officers had "finished an excellent lunch and were all seated around the table at coffee and port wine…[when] a shell had struck the roof and burst in the next room." The blast riddled the room— which both Churchill and Sinclair were using as a bedroom at night—with splinters, some of which also forced their way into the room where all were sitting.

According to McDavid, Churchill was playing with his battery-powered torch when the shell detonated. A splinter blasted straight through it. "If it had been any nearer, it certainly would have taken off his wrist," McDavid said.

McDavid himself suffered damage to the hand, apparently from shattered china. The front line troops thought it served him right for indulging in such luxuries as proper plates, Gibb wrote—meals in the trenches were eaten from metal plates and mess tins.

In his letter to Clementine the following day, Churchill requested another torch. He had put his men to building more and stronger dugouts, he said. Such was his exhaustion, he noted, that he slept that night soundly in the partially destroyed bedroom.

Grumbling from the trenches, Gibb complained that the following days saw "such a scene that must have been witnessed at the erection of the pyramids."

In charge of this labor, it seems, was Captain Ramsay—the man whom Churchill had relieved of his company after his late show at parade and who had been boasting to other officers (Gibb claims) that he had managed to cut his workload. Ramsay was kept up all hours with the building of new fortifications at the farm, Gibb says, "and a thousand times a day wished himself back in [his previous role commanding a] Company."

Churchill also had the cellars drained in some nearby buildings. They were too exposed to become his HQ, he decided, but he used the position—which he dubbed the "conning tower"—to observe the battlefield and coordinate artillery fire.

The additional work on fortifications, Gibb says, was unpopular. Overall, though, Churchill seems to have been well on his way to winning over the ordinary Fusiliers.

From the beginning, according to Gibb, many had been privately delighted to have a "celebrity," somebody recognizable they could talk of in their letters. Exactly who he was, does seem to have been less clear—many got his name wrong, calling him "Lord Churchill," 'Viscount Churchill" or even the "Duke of Churchill." Several referred to him as "Sir Winston," a title he would not in fact earn until 1953. Others were equally vague on his rank, perhaps baffled by his non-regulation clothing and unable to comprehend how such a larger-than-life character could just be a colonel. They referred to him simply as "The General."

Most of the written accounts of Churchill in the trenches inevitably come from officers. The handful of accounts from his men speak of him with almost greater reverence.

Fusilier Reginald Hurt—aged twenty in 1916—later recalled in a letter to Churchill's biographer how Churchill and Sinclair once came across him on guard in the trenches. It was a freezing night and Hurt had put down his rifle to jump up and down and keep warm. Suddenly, two figures jumped down from the top of the parapet.

"Fortunately for me and my sleeping colleagues, it was Churchill...Archibald Sinclair and not a German patrol," Hurt wrote. "The five or ten minutes that followed were amongst the unhappiest of my life, all because my rifle was not in my possession."

The reprimand, Hurt felt, was entirely justified. But on learning that he was amongst the youngest soldiers in the trenches and had been there since the age of eighteen, Churchill's "anger evaporated and he became almost paternal."

A corporal caught doing the same thing the following night was more seriously punished because he was a more experienced soldier and should have set an example, Hurt reported.

On another occasion in reserve, Hurt said Churchill intervened personally to make sure he was issued new boots after spotting him limping.

To his officers, Churchill still appeared somewhat more of a liability.

On his first nighttime foray into no man's land to visit the forward observation posts—positions forward of the front trench in the shell holes between the lines—Churchill and McDavid came under heavy machine-gun fire.

All dived for the nearest shell hole, McDavid later recalled. "Suddenly a blinding glare of light appeared from the depths of the hole and with it the CO's muffled request to 'put that bloody light out.' Seconds later, it became clear it was Churchill's own torch, inadvertently activated as he crouched in the mud.

Hakewill-Smith, the teenage regular subaltern, complained Churchill's frequent trips into no man's land were always "nerve wracking." "He was like a baby elephant," he said—too loud and showing no fear. "He never fell when a shell went off, he never went down when a bullet when past. 'It's no damn use ducking, the bullet has gone a long way past by now.'"

These displays of bravado, most concluded, were primarily for the men. "I have seen him stand on the firing point in broad daylight," McDavid told Gilbert "to encourage the jocks and prove to the man on the fire step how little danger there was."

One night, under a heavy barrage, Gibb recalled Churchill looking over the parapet and asking, "in a dreamy voice: 'Do you like War?'"

"The only thing to do was to pretend not to hear him," wrote Gibb. "At that moment I profoundly hated War. But at that and every moment, I believe Winston Churchill revelled in it. There was no such thing as fear in him."

Unsurprisingly, Churchill related few of these escapades to Clementine. He gave the impression that most of the crawling around no man's land was done by Sinclair who apparently spent considerable time outside the trenches at night exploring "like an inquisitive mongoose."

Still, he was openly critical of unnecessary risk-taking in others. On February 15, he told Clementine he had criticized his young officers after a trench-raiding party sent out to cut pieces of the German wire left a union jack flag hanging there in a sign of bravado. "Can you imagine anything so silly?" he wrote—the Germans would now be much more alert.

AS MUCH AS he could, Churchill deliberately cultivated the impression he was delighted to be commanding a battalion and no longer hankered after a brigadier general's tunic and larger formation.

In a letter to his mother in late January, he has suggested a battalion might actually suit him rather better. It was certainly a challenge.

"Commanding a Battalion is like being captain of a ship," he wrote. "This is a very searching task and a severe burden. Especially so when all the officers are young and only soldiers of a few months standing and when 100 yards away lies the line of the German Army...one would not have thought it possible a year ago to put a battalion thus composed into the line."

On January 29, he had written in a similar vein to Clementine: "I like this sort of work very much and I hope to be able to do it well."

When summoned to brigade headquarters on February 6 "to take command of the brigade," however, his heart clearly leapt.

"I thought at first that the change meant something effective," he wrote. But it transpired that the Brigadier General was simply away on sick leave and Churchill was, for the time being, the senior commanding officer in the brigade. He was just a "caretaker," a position he found most unsatisfactory.

Jack Seely—who was commanding a brigade in a neighboring sector—wrote that he believed Churchill remained deeply sore. "I have never seen him so disappointed and hurt," he had written in December.

Churchill was certainly not above occasionally mocking the man who did have the role. On one occasion, the brigade commander was visiting the forward trenches when he complained about some flaw he perceived. The conditions would not do at all, he told Churchill somewhat petulantly—they were *dangerous.*

Churchill did not miss a beat. "But you see, sir," he replied as politely as he could, "it is a most dangerous war."

They pulled out of the trenches early on February 7 to take up reserve positions in the village once again. According to the battalion war diary— now being filled in by Gibb—they had survived the whole six-day spell in the lines without a single fatality.

The shelling, however, was now relentless. On February 10, Churchill told Clementine three of his men had been walking in town when they were hit, one of them fatally. "In the last two days I have lost eight men, more than in six days in the front line," he said. The entire battalion was now down to 600 men instead of the 1,000 it should have had on paper.

The worst of it, he wrote, was that so many other units were in a similar position, the price of Asquith's reluctance to embrace outright conscription. The volunteer army raised by Kitchener in 1914—soon to be almost completely wiped out on the Somme—was gradually bleeding to death.

Such frustrations were clearly turning Churchill's mind back to politics. Promotion in Flanders, he told Clementine, looked as though it might be painfully slow.

"Haig will no doubt—if I survive—give me a brigade. But he will be chiefly concerned at the impression such an appointment will produce in the Army and he will certainly run no risks on my account. Can you blame him? We are only acquaintances."

EVEN IF THE Germans were unaware of Churchill's person in the trenches near "Plugstreet," his presence was in part responsible for the significant uptick in German shelling. Churchill was certainly not above using his position and access to call for much-greater-than-usual artillery support—and the Germans would often reply in kind.

Churchill was delighted to discover that the commander of the divisional artillery was Brigadier General Henry Hugh Tudor, a contemporary from his India days. Tudor became a regular visitor to the Fusiliers—and he and Churchill appeared to have used the battalion sector of the front as the ideal area to demonstrate their firepower.

On February 11, with the Fusiliers still theoretically in reserve, Tudor organized a massive artillery strafe on the frontline near Ploegsteert. Churchill accompanied him to the frontline trenches to watch as all the division's guns opened up on two small sections of the German frontline.

"This was very exciting," wrote Churchill, particularly when two of the shells fell short and landed in the British trenches behind.

Later that day, he found himself caught up in the German retaliation when a shell fell near divisional HQ at a nearby chateau just as he visited.

On the same excursion, Churchill and Sinclair rode into the nearby town of Amientieres. Shelling was still ongoing.

Once again, he commented on the resilience of civilians under continuous bombardment. "Every now and again a shell passed overhead," he told Clementine. "But there were a fair number of shops open with women serving in them and a lot of factories smoking away as if nothing was going on."

A photography studio was still functioning. Churchill and Sinclair were photographed together, the former "strapped up" in his waterproofs and French helmet, the younger, taller Sinclair standing beside him in his Life Guards cap. They looked like tourists, smiling for their families back home.

Two days later, they were back in the line.

THE STRAIN, CHURCHILL told Clementine on February 13, was beginning to tell. "Some of my officers have returned from leave," he wrote. "They are very homesick. No doubt they feel the weight and burden of this business and long for its conclusion. But it will take a long time and we must not expect quick results."

Churchill's own thoughts too were turning to home. Aside from a handful of days around Christmas, he had been in France since the end of November—almost three months.

He was, he told Clementine, reveling in his role. It was, he realized, almost exactly where he might have been had he never sought greatness and simply plodded forward with a straightforward army career.

"Kiss the kittens," he wrote. "I think a great deal about you all. I never expected to be so completely involved in the military machine. It almost seems as though my life in the great world was a dream and I have been moving slowly forward in the Army all these years from subaltern to colonel."

He was learning. When Tudor came round

the following day and organized yet another artillery strafe, Churchill was careful to withdraw his own troops from the most exposed positions first rather than leave them vulnerable to any German retaliation or shots that fell short.

Churchill had moved his battalion HQ to another farm in the hope of avoiding shelling. Two days later that was hit too.

SINCLAIR AND CHURCHILL had been up until 1:30 a.m. the previous night going round the trenches. On the morning of February 16, they were just finishing up their breakfast when the first German shells began to fall.

The first landed some 200 meters or so away, Churchill told Clementine later that day, and the two men decided to continue with their bacon, eggs, jam and marmalade. Seconds later, however, the building shook with another direct hit.

As they crouched outside in one of the newly constructed dugouts, another twenty or so shells slammed into the earth and outbuildings.

Once again, the bedroom Churchill shared with Sinclair was thoroughly shredded. So was the signals room, wounding signals officer Lawrence Kemp.

"It was odd gobbling bacon and marmalade in the dugout while the doctor bandaged the great raw wounds of our poor officer a foot or two away," Churchill wrote. "Archie is very good—cool, methodical, careful—yet quite fearless. I do not think I mind it very much. At any rate, it does not affect my spirits or my temper. But it is a very curious life to lead."

In a letter the following day, he went even further to assure her he was fine. "These last five days have gone like a flash," he wrote. "The complete absence of worry or strain, of mental work of any serious kind, the good food, warmth and comfort in which we live with lots of open air is very good for one's health...I expect I am putting on weight."

Just how much strain the other officers were under, however, was clear. Before being sent back to hospital to recover, the signals officer Kemp had been given the nose cone of the shell that wounded him. He was so pleased to be leaving the line, Churchill said, that he kissed it.

That night, Churchill organized a "little strafe" of the German lines in retaliation. Again, his own positions came under fire. A well-respected senior NCO was killed. It was the only fatality of the six-day spell in the trenches, he wrote, but another ten men had been wounded, mostly at headquarters.

ONCE AGAIN, THE German artillery kept up its onslaught as the Fusiliers went into reserve. Now the strain was telling on Churchill too.

"We have been hunted by shells during these two days 'in rest,'" wrote Churchill to Clementine on February 20, chiding her for only writing in one letter in five days.

He and Sinclair had been arguing over the best way to protect themselves from shellfire in their reserve billets, he wrote. Sinclair favored taking shelter in the cellar during a barrage. Churchill felt it preferable to sandbag the key rooms in which they slept and worked.

Later that day, Churchill was working in his room above the convent when shells started to fall. According to his letter to Clementine, Sinclair returned from a walk to find that one had dropped down the chimney into the cellar itself. Only by chance did it not explode and kill the occupants, who included the surviving battalion signalers as well as a local family.

"This is now the third time in a fortnight that our bedroom has been pierced by shells—three different rooms," he wrote. "I have now moved back 300 yards to the beastly little farm as I am sure they mean to smash the little town pieces."

"One lives calmly on the brink of the abyss," he continued. "But I can understand how tired people get of it if it goes on month after month. All the excitement dies away and there is only dull resentment."

In a later essay published in the 1920s, Churchill revealed just how much that barrage had shaken him. In his haste to leave the room, he believed he had left behind the document on which he was working, a report on the still highly secret tank. It took him several days to find it again, stuffed forgotten into a rarely used pocket of his jacket.

By February 22, Churchill's looming home leave was figuring ever larger in his thoughts.

"I am suddenly beginning to look forward very much to coming home," he wrote, asking Clementine to arrange visitors to come to him at Cromwell Road rather than having to go out for dinner.

Two days later, however, all leave was cancelled. "It seems that the Germans are expected to develop a great offensive against this western part quite soon," he told Clementine. If that happened, he said, then the Allies—potentially including the Fusiliers—would probably counterattack elsewhere.

The expected hammer blow never fell—at least, not on Ypres. By then, the German onslaught at Verdun was underway, the French army fighting a desperate rear-guard action to stop its line collapsing.

By February 26, the Fusiliers were back in the line. A detachment of Royal Engineers had further bolstered the defenses of battalion HQ, he reassured Clementine.

"Snow covers the ground and we do our scouting in calico gowns—almost invisible at 20 yards," he wrote. "I like this farm much better than the one where I am in 'at rest.' There are a good many things to burst a shell before it actually gets us and then the sandbags may be counted on to stop the splinters and keep out the blast. Inside we have a glowing brazier and two comfortable canvas beds. We sleep warm and peaceful."

Leave was reinstated. He would, he told Clementine, be back with her by March 2.

Chapter 6 – An Unsuccessful Leave

Clementine and Churchill had missed each other terribly. Both must have hoped his ten-day leave would give them a chance for stolen peace and intimacy. But it was simply not to be.

Throughout his time in the trenches, Churchill had kept up his almost parallel political life. He had followed newspaper cuttings almost obsessively, corresponded with most of the members of the Cabinet, demanded Clementine meet with as many others as possible.

Since late 1915, Asquith's government had been teetering on the brink of collapse, primarily on conscription. As a frontline battalion commander, Churchill was all too aware that the volunteer army was exhausted. As a politician, he wondered whether the dispute might speed him back to power.

Throughout January and February, Clementine had tried to keep his ambitions—and his bitterness towards Asquith—reined in. She warned him against revealing them to passing acquaintances in the trenches, suggesting he used Archie Sinclair and family members as a "safety valve."

Terrified though she was that he might be killed, she was already trying to caution him against returning too soon. His decision to leave the government for military service, she fervently believed, would ultimately play off politically—but only if he did not come back too soon.

She was more than aware of the risks involved. At Churchill's insistence, Jock McDavid had stayed at Cromwell Road after his injury. (Clementine pronounced him a "nice boy...very small and young rather lovable" and said she felt sorry for his mother.) His accounts of the bombardment and conditions at the frontline—together with Churchill's own letters— left her little room to overly romanticize the war. But she was keenly aware of the patriotic mood at home—and the lack of sympathy there would be for a politician seen to have shirked his duty once in uniform.

"When it is all over," she had written to him in January, "we should be proud that you were a soldier and not a politician for the greater part of the war. Soldiers and soldiers' wives now seem to me the only real people."

Churchill's frustrations, however, grew ever deeper. The War Office, he felt, was moving far too slowly in the development of the tank. Not enough was being done to win control of the air.

Clementine had endured some deeply uncomfortable dinners with Asquith, apparently unsure how justified her husband's anger towards him was. The Prime Minister, for his part, seemed deeply concerned to hear of Churchill's life in the trenches.

"He *wanted* the answers to be reassuring and my good manners as a guest forbade me to make him uncomfortable which I could have of course have done," she wrote. Had she depicted him in terrible conditions, she believed, it would have put the Prime Minister off his dinner and she would not have been invited back.

Churchill's official biographer Martin Gilbert—who interviewed Clementine on several occasions towards the end of her life—believed she was never truly certain just how much Churchill's enmity towards Asquith was justified. She kept the channels of communication open.

Lloyd George, meanwhile, she never trusted. Nor was she keen on Admiral of the Fleet Jackie Fisher, the former First Sea Lord with whom Churchill had had such a tempestuous relationship and whose breakdown and resignation had helped bring her husband down.

NOW OUT OF office in London, Fisher was emerging as a new center of political opposition to Asquith. As late as February 2, Churchill had been worrying that the Prime Minister might bring the old admiral back. "Fisher without me to manage him would be disastrous," he had written to Clementine.

In that month at the front, however, his attitude seems to have softened dramatically. Gibb writes that Churchill always spoke warmly of Fisher. The truth, though, was that he saw him as a route back to power.

Fisher was a remarkably effective political operator, writing near continuous letters to newspaper editors and ministers with his trademark capital letters and italics. He was now increasingly convinced, he told others, that only Churchill could lead a credible opposition.

In the trenches, Churchill's mind had been ticking. A *Daily Mail* article had suggested him as a potential prime minister. Reports from Germany talked of rejoicing at Churchill's removal from office. Surely that meant Britain, he felt, would now welcome his return.

To his men—save perhaps Sinclair—

Churchill seems to have said nothing. If anything, his letters home in late February mentioned politics less than usual. His political supporters and allies in London told him the Prime Minister was as firmly ensconced as ever.

WHEN CHURCHILL CROSSED to England on the evening of March 2 it is not clear he had much political activity planned. He only discovered on his arrival that a parliamentary debate on the Naval Estimates was scheduled for March 7. Almost immediately, he determined to speak at it.

On March 3, a Friday, he rehearsed his speech at a dinner given by his mother. It listed a variety of his frustrations and it was well received. It made no mention of Fisher at all.

The prime minister's daughter, Violet Asquith—now Violet Bonham-Carter after marriage—later wrote she heard from others that Churchill found himself hailed as a potential man of the moment, the right person to tie together a disunited opposition. The next day, Clementine was horrified to discover Fisher had been invited to lunch.

According to F.E. Smith, after the lunch she took Fisher aside. "Keep your hands off my husband", she is supposed to have said. "You have all but ruined him once. Leave him alone now."

On March 5, however, the two men met again. Churchill had decided to add a dramatic conclusion to his speech. He would demand the return of Fisher to the Admiralty. In doing so, he hoped, he would prove once and for all that he had risen above petty jealousies.

Given the letter below, sent by Fisher to Churchill the following day, it is hard to see why he should have trusted the erratic admiral's judgment. But the two men, it seemed, had made up their minds.

"Proof of YOUR SOLE OBJECT BEING THE WAR will have (*justly*) an *immense* effect on your popularity," Fisher wrote. "Ride on the crest of that Popularity…the reason the Government are strong is THERE IS NO OPPOSITION LEADER! *…you can be Prime Minister if you like!*"

The night before the speech, the Asquiths dined at Cromwell Road. Margot Asquith sat next to Churchill. According to her daughter Violet later, she told him what a "fine exit" he had made in foregoing politics for the trenches. "Don't go and spoil it all," she said.

Churchill, apparently, had a glint in his eyes. He made it clear he would speak the following day but gave no details. He did ask Margot, though, whether the country might benefit from a strong opposition and who might lead it. Margot was sure, Violet wrote, that Churchill was "dreaming of an amazing opposition that he might lead."

Opposition leaders, of course, might often go further. If anything, Churchill's time in the trenches had left him more convinced than ever that he was the ideal wartime leader for Britain. But it was—for that conflict at least—nothing but a pipedream. The Conservatives and Liberals, the two largest parties, were already in coalition. Any opposition would be limited to the still fledgling Labour Party and whatever independents it could attract.

When he had last crossed the floor in 1911,

Churchill had been riding the political moment. This time he was out of touch and probably still seriously exhausted. Clementine thought he was making a terrible mistake. He ignored her. Barely a week earlier, he had been enduring shelling in Belgium. Now he was convinced his hour had come.

Churchill met *Manchester Guardian* editor C.P. Snow on the morning of the speech on May 7. Snow noted Churchill "felt he was in for a serious enterprise." The speech he was about to make, Churchill said, required more courage than anything in the trenches.

IT WAS A disaster. Churchill's suggestion of reappointing the aging admiral with whom he himself had been unable to work was met with open surprise and ridicule.

That single point completely overshadowed all his more reasonable ideas and criticisms: greater resources to fight the submarine menace, more aircraft and other equipment. Once again, he had made himself appear too impetuous, too hungry for glory.

It was almost the opposite of the image he had worked so hard to create in the Fusiliers, that of a mature, responsible commander who took no unnecessary risks.

It does not seem to have been immediately obvious to Churchill just how badly he had miscalculated, even with the jeers and catcalls in the House. He had, after all, just delivered one of the most potent attacks on the government in parliament of the entire war so far. And he had done so in a country where discontent and frustration at the conflict were increasingly open and widespread.

He left the House immediately after the speech, so missed the litany of MPs afterwards who decried it and spoke of the dangers should he influence imperial policy again.

"We wish him well in France," said MP and former Admiral Hedworth Meux at the end of a vitriolic speech. "And hope that he will stay there."

BEFORE THE SPEECH, Churchill had talked openly of extending his leave to talk at the Army Estimates the following week. They, he hoped, would give him another chance to lambast the government and secure his position as its pre-eminent critic. Now he could not make up his mind whether to stay or return to the trenches.

On March 8, Fisher came by Cromwell Street to persuade him to continue. Clementine was strongly against it. That afternoon, Churchill's replacement as First Lord of the Admiralty Arthur Balfour replied to his speech in the Commons, attacking its author with yet more scorn and ridicule.

"I cannot follow the workings of my Right Honourable Friend's mind," he said. "I should regard myself as contemptible beyond the power of expression should I yield an inch to a demand of such a kind made in such a way."

This time, Churchill was there to hear it. His response was lackluster at best, defensive and—particularly for one of the twentieth century's great orators—strikingly lacking in impact.

Still, he believed strongly his criticisms of war

policy were valid, even if he had given his foes an easy political win with the Fisher suggestion. He wrote to Kitchener at the War Office saying he wished for his leave to be extended and to be relieved of his command with the Fusiliers as soon as possible.

That afternoon, Violet Bonham-Carter met him at his mother's house. She later recalled that he looked "pale, defined, on the defensive. I shall never forget the pain of the talk which followed."

He seemed, she said, almost completely defeated. Still, he said he had decided it was better to remain in London and use what political influence he had from there.

By now, Asquith had secured Fisher's silence by flattery and by inviting him to the War Council (although the Admiral would never hold real power again). Now, the Prime Minister met with Churchill.

Churchill's father, Lord Randolph, Asquith reminded him, had thrown away his political career over a relative trifle on military expenditure. He had resigned from the government on almost a whim and never returned. He hoped Churchill would avoid a similar mistake by staying to challenge the government.

Asquith told his daughter that Churchill had tears in his eyes as he departed and he was sure he would return to France.

On March 10, the plans for a new opposition received an unexpected boost when an independent MP beat both main parties in a by-election. Fisher and *Daily Telegraph* editor Garvin went to Churchill to encourage him to continue. Churchill began rehearsing a speech for the Army Estimates debate.

Churchill and Fisher were still having

meetings. Churchill had won from the Prime Minister a written assurance that if he returned to the trenches now, he could still return easily at a future date without opposition.

In the short term, though, Clementine persuaded him it would be best to go back to his battalion. Churchill told supporters he expected to be back in London within the week. Clementine accompanied him to Dover, spending the night in a hotel with him before he sailed on March 12.

AS CHURCHILL HAD seen with his officers, returning to the trenches from home could be bruising and traumatic.

He had gone from expecting a quiet break to being persuaded he was on the threshold of greatness. Now he appeared more politically isolated than even after Gallipoli. He believed the war was being desperately mismanaged and there seemed nothing he could do about it.

Alternatively, he was turning his back on what should be his moment, letting down all of those he could help if only he clung on and fought. He had urgent decisions to make and little energy left with which to make them.

From Dover, he sent a letter to Asquith resigning once again. He gave Clementine a statement to be given the Press Association explaining his decision. Then he had changed his mind and telegraphed Asquith to withdraw the letter. The relieved Prime Minister sent his son-in-law racing round Cromwell Road to make sure Clementine did not issue the statement in error.

On top of everything else, Churchill knew he had clearly seriously upset his wife.

On March 16, he wrote to Clementine from Soyer's Farm, the now heavily sandbagged settlement the battalion used as a reserve position now that central "Plugstreet" was so badly shelled.

"I'm still considering my course," he wrote, adding that there seemed to be nothing lost through delay now that the Army Estimates debate was passed. "That it is right for me to come home is certain. What is not clear is when and on what grounds. It is worth studying this a little longer."

He had been discussing the matter with the divisional commander, Lieutenant General Furse, he said. Like many others, he felt Churchill could achieve more in London: "He had no doubts my duty was at home," Churchill wrote after the meeting. "Although it may be easier for you here with a battalion or a brigade and pleasanter, you have no right to think of that," he quoted Furse as saying.

Archie Sinclair, however, had sided with Clementine. "Archie is a strong advocate of my stay here…[until] there is some definite reason for a break. He is a great comfort to me out here. It is odd how similar are the standpoints from which you both view my troublesome affairs."

The Germans shelled the town all day, he said. Many of the Fusiliers had sat or stood in the entrance to their dugouts and simply watched the mayhem "as though it were some splendid joke." Trucks and transport widens were still passing along the road, sometimes missed only by a few yards, he said.

"Archie was particularly unfeeling and I

rebuked him," Churchill continued. "But, after all, at any moment the guns might have turned onto us…So people feel it is all in a day's work."

That Sunday, he said, he had organized another concert for the men including the services of the divisional band. As well as he was keeping them happy, however, he was very aware he'd fallen short in other areas.

"Don't be unduly anxious," he wrote. "Tender love, my dearest soul. I cannot tell you how much I treasure and count on you…it was hard on you to set you such exhausting tasks. You discharged them famously."

There was something else he had forgotten in London, he noted. He was almost out of pen nibs.

MARCH 17 WAS MUCH quieter. "Not a single shell," Churchill wrote. "My conviction strengthens and deepens each day that my place is there…Meanwhile, the actual step seems so easy to pull off [and] so irrevocable when taken that I continue to pause on the break.

"Could I help to a victorious peace more in the House of Commons than here? That is the sole question. Believe me, if my life could materially aid our fortunes I would not grudge it."

That evening, Churchill and Sinclair took a walk along the lines to the neighboring sector. By the following day, Churchill had made a decision.

Sinclair, he told Clementine, was "very much run down." Perhaps his "unfeeling" attitude during the artillery barrage was a sign of exhaustion. Either way, leave had been reopened and Sinclair was due for some. Churchill would stay with the battalion at least until he came back.

"It would have been very hard on him to cut him off from his longed for holiday," Churchill wrote, adding that he wanted the parentless Sinclair to stay with Clementine at Cromwell Road "and for you and [sister-in-law] Goonie to cherish him and nourish him. He is all alone in the world and very precious as a friend to me."

FOR CHURCHILL, THE spell without Sinclair was amongst the hardest. Even more than after Gallipoli, he was questioning his own judgment, his purpose, his never-ending quest for power and influence.

On March 20, the Fusiliers moved back into the trenches. A new brigadier general had been appointed his immediate superior: Gerald Trotter, future military attaché to Washington D.C. Trotter was a vast improvement on his predecessor, Churchill told Clementine—but the fact he was given a job that could have gone to Churchill "clearly shows that I have no prospects."

"I do not mind...If I were to stay here, I could hardly be better suited than where I am," he wrote. He was still determined to return, he continued, simply awaiting guidance in letters he expected from his handful of political allies and his Dundee constituency agent.

The most important thing, he told Telegraph editor J.L. Garvin, was that he return "under good conditions," leaving the front for good reason.

The weather, he told Clementine, had

changed for the worse, "but the farm is very comfortable and well supplied and the enemy have left us alone for some days."

On March 22, he sketched out again to a skeptical Clementine his arguments for returning. "I shall have served for nearly five months of the front, almost always in the frontline, certainly without discredit discharging arduous and difficult duties to the full satisfaction of my superiors and the advantage of my officers and men," he wrote. "I have a recognised position in British politics…enabling me to command the attention (at any rate) of my fellow countrymen in a manner not exceeded by more than three or four living men."

But it would be better, he said, to have "some local reason for a break such as our division going out of the line…but this advantage must be weighed against opportunities in England. I cannot decide yet."

His March 23 letter is largely devoid of military details. He had written separately to Sinclair on "our military shop," he said, and Sinclair could tell her. He believed he had identified a potential replacement for himself to lead the battalion, he added, a major who had been with them at the beginning of the war.

"This letter therefore is only to tell you of my love and faith in you and my devotion to you and our darling kittens," he wrote. "I reproach myself so much with having got so involved in politics when I was home that all the comfort and joy of our meeting was spoiled."

Reconciling their public and private lives, he said, was always going to be difficult. "But next time I come home, it will be with a set purpose and vehicles and with no wild and anxious hurry of fleeting moments and uncertain plans.

"I'm going to live calmly. Two more days in the trenches, then 700 yards back to another farm—the one I like. Well, I like this place too. What is left of it."

"I am struck by Archie's appearance," Clementine wrote on March 22. "He looks pale and careworn. He cares for you so much and takes your affairs to heart I think."

THE REST OF Churchill's letters from March keep up that deeply introspective tone. They show a man reevaluating his life, purpose, wants.

On March 23, Ulster Unionist MP Edward Carson—the closest thing Britain had to an opposition leader—wrote to Churchill giving his views on his situation.

"I think myself, speaking quite candidly, that having stated in your resignation you were going to take out active duty in the field it will give lots of grounds for criticism if you come back without the opportunity of showing the grave necessity you feel for such a step," he wrote. "I say all this in order that you may consider the possibility in the near future of a better opportunity of returning that just now."

The Fusiliers moved back into reserve on March 27. The next night, Churchill dined with another general who, he said, repeated more or less word for word the advice of Carson's letter. As he rode home, he told Clementine, "the sky was flickering with artillery but no sound made its way against the prevailing wind."

On March 25, Clementine had written frankly of her worries over the marriage. "When next I see you, I hope so there will be a little time for us both alone," she wrote. "We are still young but Time flies stealing love away and leaving only friendship which is very peaceful but not stimulating or warming."

Churchill was at pains to reassure her she was more than a friend, confidant or secretary.

"Oh my Darling do not write of 'friendship' to me—I love you more each month that passes and feel the need of you and all your beauty," he wrote. "I too feel sometimes the longing for rest and peace. So much effort, so many years of ceaseless fighting and worry…"

His thoughts too were turning to the passage of time and what really mattered, he said. "Is it 40 and finished?" he asked. For almost the first time, it seems, he was tempted by something other than greatness, power or glory.

"Would it not be delicious to go for a few weeks to some lovely spot in Italy or Spain to wander about together in bright warm sunlight far from the clash of arms or bray of Parliaments? We know each other so well now and could play better than we ever could."

Was that a reference to sex? I rather think it was.

He would not particularly mind dying, he told her, if he could meet her in another life and "pay you all the love and honour of the great romances." Two days earlier, he said, shells had been falling nearby and it had not made him jump at all.

"But I felt that 20 yards more to the left and

no more tangles to unravel, no more anxieties to face, no more hatred and injustices to encounter. Joy to my foes…a good ending to a chequered life, a final gift— undervalued to an ungrateful country—and impoverishment of the warmaking power of Britain which no one would ever know or measure or mourn."

But he would not give up, he continued. "I am going on fighting to the very end in any station open to me from which I can most effectively drive the war to victory."

The ludicrousness of the world seemed to be striking him. A handful of survivors from Ernest Shackleton's expedition to the South Pole had just reached land. A rescue mission was being launched to the Antarctic to bring back the rest. With the world in flames, he said, it seemed ridiculous. "But I suppose something will have to be done."

Shortly after, he reopened the letter to add a postscript. Two red Tamworth pigs he had mentioned a month or so earlier had survived against the odds, he wrote, and were visiting his dugout. Another postscript later talked of "quite a good mouse" reconnoitering the floor of the cave "with the utmost skill."

MARCH 30 WAS CHURCHILL'S last night on his own without Sinclair. Two days earlier he had received a letter from his constituency agent George Ritchie. Like almost everyone else, he was advising Churchill to hurry less in his return to London. "I think it is worthy of your consideration…whether it is worth to put a weapon in the hands of your enemies that would hold a charge of instability at you," he wrote.

By now, though, Churchill was feeling much more stable. Clementine was complaining of one of her occasional bouts of bronchitis. He told her to take it easy.

"There are very long waits at here with nothing to do," he wrote. "They have just begun to shell a little town. The shells come overhead, pass and burst 100 yards away. I am going to put on my helmet and go outside where I can see them."

Chapter 7 – Final Days

By early April, it was clear that Churchill's time in the trenches was coming to an end.

"I am simply living here from day to day pending the result of some enquiries I am making," he told his mother in a letter on April 3. "It is only a matter of how and when."

The weather was improving, he told Clementine the same day. He had now been commanding the Battalion for exactly three months and they were back once again in the trenches.

The shelling seemed lighter, he said, but random death remained close. In a letter to Lord Curzon, he thanked him for a shipment of brandy which "was a great solace." One bottle, however, had been smashed by a shell "which also killed three men just outside the little room in which I gave you tea."

The sheer range and number of Churchill's visitors—whether in the trenches or in reserve—remained a subject or fascination for the rest of the battalion.

The previous brigade commander had been remarkably unliked ("I once thought I'd look him up after the war and declare another war on him on my own account," Gibb wrote). His successor, Trotter, was a popular visitor. Artillery Brigadier General Tudor was often there as well as the divisional commander Major General Furse. So, inevitably, was Jack Seely and many of his Canadians.

On one occasion, Seely himself sang and played the piano at one of Churchill's several concert parties. "The men were very pleased with the performance and not a little surprised to find the General from whose company it was possible to derive some slight pleasure," wrote Gibb.

On one occasion towards the end of Churchill's time in the trenches, Gibb says, their tiny farm played host to multiple distinguished generals at once. As the dinner drew to a close, he recalled Churchill turning to one of them "in the blandest manner."

Would the general like to see his trenches, he asked. The general replied that he would. So did another.

"We'll all go, then," Churchill said. "It's a lovely night, though very quiet. We might get out at the front."

And with that blithe pledge to take them out of the trenches into no man's land itself, Churchill led them down towards the front line.

The perception amongst the frontline soldiers, Gibb said, was that most senior staff officers tended to dislike the trenches and avoid them when possible.

This, he felt, was actually unfair—in fact, losses amongst generals and staff officers in the First World War were as high as in the second. The battalion itself was used to seeing the divisional commander, Lieutenant General Furse, in the frontline frequently including on reconnaissance into no man's land.

Still, the Fusiliers loved the spectacle.

"The Battalion was delighted with this performance," writes Gibb. "It was a great joke to the jaded infantry to see them all out there tearing their breeches and thumbs on the wire, wallowing in mud and cursing over clothes that had never been grovelled in before."

On April 6, Churchill wrote to Clementine that the German shelling had again increased. Most of the weight fell on units to the north, he said, but the previous day an officer and six men had been wounded when his forward trenches were hit. An officer visiting from another battalion was killed.

"I have now had about 100 killed and wounded in this regiment since coming into the line which is about one in five of those exposed in the trenches," he wrote, reflecting that this was nothing unusual amongst front-line units. "This drain must amount to a lot spread over the whole immense front. I hope the Germans suffer equally."

He had become entirely used to casualties, shells and bullets, he wrote, adding that they "seem to lose their significance. But I suppose they hit just as hard."

For his own mental health, Churchill kept up his newly acquired hobby of painting. Two of his works from the trenches survive at his country house in Chartwell.

One shows an artillery barrage falling on Ploegsteert. The second, by far the more striking, is the courtyard at one of the battalion farms. It's a stark, almost brutal picture of the ruined place which had become the center of their world.

CHURCHILL'S SOCIALISING WITH top commanders was in part deeply political. Having determined he wished to return home, he was keen to get as much insight as possible into their complaints over the conduct of the war so far.

In particular, senior and junior officers alike were increasingly frustrated by the failure of the Asquith government to introduce compulsory widespread conscription. By returning to Parliament, even in the backbenches, he hoped he could act as a voice for those concerns, furthering his own interests at the same time.

Opposition leader Carson told Churchill by letter he believed the government might fall over the issue at a debate in Parliament. Churchill began stealing his attendance, arguing that on this issue all MPs serving with the military should be recalled from France for the debate.

Clementine, however, remained convinced Churchill should not return too soon.

It was, of course, a different time. In her letter of April 1, she recounted reading in the *Times* of the various Victoria Cross and other decorations awarded for bravery. "There was a long list of heroic actions," she wrote. "What a heroic age we live in."

But she remained starkly aware of the risks and of what she stood to lose.

"Dear Winston I am so torn and lacerated over you," she wrote on April 6. "If I say 'stay where you are' a wicked bullet may find you where you might but for me escape."

To be truly great, she told him, his actions must be understandable "by simple people." His Fisher speech had failed because it was not an easy argument to understand. "It required another speech to make it clear. I do long to see you terribly. Your last visit was no help to me personally. I must see you soon."

The accounts of Gibb and others make no

mention of Churchill's endless deliberations on politics. In his letter of April 7 to Clementine, Churchill revealed he had deliberately kept them in the dark.

"I have never discussed my going home with them but I'm sure they think I should do so," he wrote, adding that he was hugely touched by the displays of the loyalty to him of officers and men alike. "The men put up my photograph in the trenches and I'm sure they would make an effort if I ask them and some big test came upon us. I have worked very hard to maintain discipline without severity."

ON THE SUBJECT of military discipline, however, Gibb makes it clear that some of the other officers—including himself—did differ sharply from Churchill. They felt he was far too lenient.

"The line which he took would be bound to shock the regular soldier," he wrote, adding that while sometimes this was no bad thing, "it is difficult to see how his ideas on the matter could receive sanction without serious detriment to the one essential of discipline, prompt obedience to orders."

If a soldier refused an order given to him by an NCO, Gibb said, it was impossible to get Churchill to punish him as seriously as would have happened in most other units. Instead, he would tend to explain the rules again to the offenders and give him a chance to mend his ways. It was, Gibb said, not always entirely effective. "I'm afraid the men began to realise that they might at least once indulge themselves in the luxury of telling their sergeants to go to hell," he recalled.

Still, he says— and perhaps in part as a direct result—Churchill had by this stage become very popular throughout the battalion.

In the officers' mess at night, he would willingly regale all with stories of his time in government. He was always generally warm in his endorsement of political figures of the era, Gibb said, including those such as Fisher who were periodic enemies.

His bitterness towards Asquith, Gibb said, was noted but "was in no way surprising to anyone in the line in 1916: it was merely endorsement by an insider of the feelings of most of us."

Churchill was so sufficiently generous in sharing his luxuries, he continued, that they did not spark the resentment that they could have done.

"Had he not been so decent about it we should have been annoyed by that tin bath of the colonel's," he wrote. "It was a thing like a greatly magnified soap dish but it was possible to have a very good bath in it. Many one I had, as had most of us."

That, it seems, included at least some of the private soldiers. Watt recalls several of the privates acting as batmen to the officers would often be found waiting outside the reserves building that housed it, ready to take their turn.

Two of them, Blackwood and Martin, were the "comedians of the place," Gibb wrote. The former was a diminutive Lowland Scot and the latter a six-foot-six Cockney. "It is unfortunate that no approximation to a report of one of their terms can be given. Their language was too horrifying."

Churchill kept up his habit of visiting the front-line positions often even late at night and under fire.

When men were wounded, Churchill was often there, providing comfort and aid. This approach contrasted sharply with Commander-in-Chief Douglas Haig, who was encouraged by his staff officers to stop visiting wounded as he found it so upsetting.

"It did not matter where he was or what he was doing, if he heard that a man was wounded he [Churchill] set off at once to see him," Gibb wrote.

"It always struck me that Colonel Churchill achieved in a remarkable measure success in dealing with the rank and file of his battalion," he added. "His attitude towards the men was ideally sympathetic and not marked by that condescending *hauteur* which goes so far to frustrate the efforts of a number of our regular officers."

Churchill's own personal batman, Charles Arthur Whiting, told the BBC in the 1960s that he was always extremely friendly.

Whiting's duties, he said, included keeping Churchill's personal kit clean, polishing his boots and buttons. "Brush him down like a horse, you know. Brush him down and make him look smart and everything."

"A very friendly man indeed," he said. "He knew we were there for the war and we [had] got to behave ourselves and he will always give you a laugh at anything like that. He'd always make things come right."

According to Gibb, Churchill would make a point of addressing each new detachment of soldiers as they arrived. They would be lined up outside his headquarters to be welcomed, lectured and introduced to the battalion.

"In the evening just after dark there was always a nice little concert of rifle and machine-gun bullets mewing and zipping among the splintered roofs and the thatch," he wrote. "I think that most of the men would have let him say anything if only they could have been assured they had not really been lined up to be shot."

ON APRIL 7, CHURCHILL related to Clementine his desperate last-minute efforts to send her birthday wishes six days earlier. Clearly, he had pulled every string at his disposal: motorcycle couriers, telephones and military signalers.

On April 10, he wrote more harshly. "You are deluded if you think that by remaining here and doing nothing I shall recover my influence in affairs," he said. "On the other hand I must be very careful in all I do and how I do it."

The same day, he wrote to Lloyd George saying he intended to return to London shortly "and I am only delaying from day to day on account of small ties here which are being adjusted."

On April 14, he told Clementine the Fusiliers were moving back into the line for another six days. There was little prospect of any immediate rest, he said—the BEF was taking over ever more of the front from the French as they attempted to reinforce the growing battle at Verdun.

The Fusiliers and their wider division, he said, were now so depleted and exhausted it was hard to imagine them being put on the offensive. British artillery fire in the sector was also much reduced by the need to conserve ammunition for other current and future battles.

In his early days on the line, Churchill had been heavily dependent on his deputy Sinclair. Now the relationship seemed reversed. Increasingly, Churchill reported, he himself was the only one who could be relied on to "play war with a smile."

"Archie is much burdened by the war and is so much older and duller," Churchill wrote, noting that Sinclair had now been in the trenches twenty months. "I am left to supply the spirits of the mess which I do nine times out of ten with chaff and chatter."

That night, Churchill took Sinclair to dinner in the still often-shelled Amentieres. "I succeeded in cheering him up…he is most courageous, conscientious and hard-working but he hates every hour of it with a profound loathing."

"I am not like this," Churchill told Clementine the next day. "When I am not consumed with inward fury at the damnable twists with which I have been served and chewing black charcoal with all my might, I am buoyant and lively and none of them but Archie knows or guesses what I feel."

The Germans were firing into the nearby woods with a much heavier artillery piece, he said.

IN FRANCE, CHURCHILL was being told by ever more fellow officers that he should return home and take up the political fight on their behalf. On April 21, Churchill's divisional commander Major

General Furse wrote to him that he was granted leave to return home for the debate called by opposition frontbencher Carlson on compulsory military service.

"The present political situation amazes me," Furse wrote. "How anyone—however clever—can suppose that a Cabinet is capable of winning this war for the British Empire when it cannot agree on a definite policy on how the Army is to be maintained…passes my comprehension."

Shortly after Churchill departed for London for the conscription debate, Sinclair wrote from the trenches making it clear that he too believed Churchill's "true war station" was in Parliament on the opposition benches. "*Do* come and say goodbye to everybody," he said.

Churchill had made clear his wish that Sinclair return with him to London as a political assistant. But despite the strain, Sinclair told him he would rather remain at the front.

"I can't believe that it can be right for me, young, physically fit and unwounded to leave the field at this juncture," he said in a letter on April 25, the day of the debate.

Victory, he said, would require every man to "strain every nerve, brace every sinew and concentrate…on doing his best to beat the Bosch. We must each apply this test to ourselves. Accordingly, you must return to Parliament and I must obviously stay here."

AS THE APRIL 25 Commons debate was held in secret, no verbatim copy or transcript exists. Clementine believed that had it been reported publicly, it would have gone much of the way to rehabilitating his reputation in public and undoing the damage of the "Fisher speech."

With discussions ongoing, Churchill cabled his commanders in Flanders to request a further extension of his leave. The suggestion, however, was vetoed. The Corps Commander, Lt. Gen Fergusson, later explained to Churchill he felt it unacceptable for him to be pursuing a simultaneous political career while still being personally responsible for a battalion in the trenches.

That situation, however, was already drawing to a close. On his return to the trenches on April 29, Churchill told his wife it seemed inevitable that the 6th Battalion Royal Scots Fusiliers would be broken up. It had lost too many men to be viable.

Their latest stint in the trenches, he said, was likely to be their last. If there were to be no delays in that process, he would seek a permanent return to London.

"All is fairly quiet here though we have had a few casualties from shelling," he finished.

His April 30 letter focused mainly on politics, particularly his regret at not being able to further chastise the Asquith government after what appeared to have been yet another inconclusive debate on introducing full conscription.

A considerable artillery barrage was hitting the front lines to the north, he said, along with a gas attack. Fusiliers positions were also being hit and the battalion taking further casualties. He had requested retaliation from the British guns.

The next night he provided further details. Some 500 to 600 shells had been fired at his part of the British sector. However, "we have been so crafty in distributing our men and the trenches are so well made that we had only one officer and five men wounded." Still, the Battalion's total losses killed and wounded in a six-day period alone stood at seventeen, he said.

On May 2, he told Clementine he would be heading to GHQ at St. Omer the following day to make arrangements for the future of his various officers. "The Battalion will by then have ceased to exist," he continued, making it clear this allowed finally his return to London without prejudice. It was, he said, "a most fortunate and natural conclusion."

"The Germans have just thrown 30 shells at our farm, hitting it four times but no one has been hurt," he said. "This is, I trust, a parting salute."

Epilogue

ACCORDING TO GIBB, the last few days of the battalion's existence passed in administrative chaos. They moved back from the line into billets—where, once again, they were inevitably visited by a plethora of senior officers and generals.

There was a Battalion photograph in which Churchill—almost for the first time—wore the traditional Glengarry bonnet of the regiment. There was a hugely noisy dinner. Throughout it all, Churchill focused heavily on finding new postings for the officers left without roles by the upcoming regimental merger.

On the day of departure, Churchill called one last meeting. He had come, he said, to regard the Scottish soldiers under his command as "a most formidable fighting animal."

Gibb had been nervously preparing a speech all day. He said, he later wrote, what he believed everyone else was thinking. "I believe every man felt Winston Churchill leaving us as a real personal loss."

At the same time, though, other thoughts were also passing through his head. That final regimental photo, he mused good-humoredly, had seemed all wrong. Churchill and Sinclair, he felt, were not real Scots. Sinclair in particular might be from Scotland, but his political soul was focused further south.

Scotland had given too much in the trenches, he felt. Once the war was over, he would try to do something about it.

CHURCHILL RETURNED TO London on May 7. But his initial months back in England were profoundly frustrating.

Conscription passed into law without the collapse of the Asquith government. He busied himself preparing Commons speeches in which he lambasted the government and criticized its handling of all aspects of the war.

"We must make out our minds that there is no chance of our winning in 1916," he had written to Clementine from the trenches on August 14. "That is the beginning of wisdom."

The only sensible option for Britain, he said, was to conserve its forces and prepare for a major offensive the following year.

It was a remarkably prescient letter—and an argument he would push in Parliament throughout May and June. But it was largely ignored.

In July, Britain began its offensive on the Somme, hoping to draw pressure away from the French at Verdun. It was as catastrophic as Loos but on a much larger scale: 57,000 British casualties on the first day, almost 20,000 killed. In total, more than 600,000 Allied personnel would lose their lives before it petered out several months later.

Churchill kept pushing for the technology he believed could change the game, particularly the tank. They finally entered service in force at Cambrai the following year, briefly breaking the German lines before technical failure stumped that offensive too.

From Parliament, he did what he could to push the case of those in the trenches. He tried to push for more meaningful decorations and medals for ordinary soldiers, to highlight the vast divide between conditions at the front and for staff officers and others well behind the lines.

"I do not believe the people in this country have any comprehension," he said in a July debate, "what the men in the trenches and those who are engaged in battle are doing or what their suffering and achievements are."

His political clout was less than he had hoped—and old issues kept taunting him. In an early debate, an Irish nationalist MP shouted out, "What about the Dardanelles?"

Banishing those ghosts, Churchill quickly realized, would be vital to reestablishing his reputation. While he was unsuccessful in persuading Asquith to release the official documents that showed him arguing for more troops, he was able to help force an official Commission of Enquiry.

Asquith eventually stood down as prime minister in December 1916, replaced by Lloyd George. Still, there was no place for Churchill. He began to regret his time in the trenches, believing otherwise he might still be closer to power.

That month, Sinclair wrote asking if he was considering a return to the trenches. The reply was bitter. His time there, Churchill said, had proved a "costly excursion." Had he remained at the Duchy of Lancaster instead "and shut my mouth and drawn my salary, I should today be one of the principal personages in the direction of affairs." Only if he was certain no other political progress was possible, he said, would he return to that "refuge."

In March 1917, the Dardanelles Commission issued its report, largely clearing Churchill of responsibility for its failure. Two months later, he was

sent to France to liaise with French forces in his first
official commission for the government in two years.
In July, he rejoined the Cabinet as Minister for
Munitions.

CHURCHILL'S MUCH IMPROVED grasp
of the realities of life and war was quickly apparent.
Within days, he had largely resolved a long-running
industrial dispute on the Clyde. Shortly afterwards, he
had a plan to dramatically streamline the ministry's
offices. By October, he was giving strategic advice to
Lloyd George after the Italian defeat at Caparetto.

When women munition workers demanded
better pay and conditions, Churchill backed them and
told the government the requests were entirely
reasonable. He successfully persuaded them he was
on their side and got them too back to work.

He spent considerable amounts of time in
France and Flanders, meeting both with British
commanders and the French to ascertain what was
needed and how fast. In January 1918, he visited his
old positions at Ploegsteert.

"Everything has been torn to pieces and the
shelling is at all times severe," he wrote to
Clementine. "The British line has moved forward
about a mile but all my old farms are mere heaps of
brick and mouldering sandbags."

The dugouts built at Lawrence Farm had
survived, however, he said, and were still in use. So
were the drained cellars at the convent and the
position he called the "conning tower."

In March, Churchill was in France when the
Germans began their last great offensive. In the days

that followed, he persuaded new mission workers to give up their Easter break to supply sufficient shells.

Lloyd George had him shuttle back and forth from London, delivering his personal insights on the battle. Churchill toured the trenches with French Prime Minister Georges Clemenceau, often under shellfire. Gradually, the German advance ran out of steam.

As late as June it looked as though Paris might fall. By August, however, the Allies were on the offensive. Churchill was focused on providing enough shells for 1919, the first year in which it was thought victory might be possible. But the German lines were collapsing faster than anyone expected.

As the Armistice came into effect at 11 a.m. on November 11, Churchill stood in his office in Whitehall. As he looked up the street, he saw people pouring out from every office building, he later wrote.

Clementine, only a week from the birth of her fourth child, joined him. They drove together to Downing Street to congratulate Lloyd George. On the way, the car was mobbed by jubilant crowds.

For more than four years, all of Churchill's energies had been devoted to war. Now it was over. He began to think how munitions factories might be converted, their factory workers employed.

"Is this the end?" he recalled thinking nine years later. "Is it to be merely a chapter in a cruel and senseless story? ...Will our children bleed and gasp again in devastated lands? Or will there spring from the fires of conflict...reconciliation?"

Of all the Cabinet ministers who had started the war, only Churchill and Lloyd George remained in office. Lloyd George wanted the Kaiser hanged,

Germany punished.

Churchill favored a different approach. A stable and prosperous Germany, he believed, was the best guarantor of a lasting peace.

ON THAT SCORE, he was to be disappointed. The Treaty of Versailles would impose a harsh victor's settlement. But he was back at the heart of politics.

In January 1919, he was appointed Secretary of State for War. Now his responsibility was overseeing the mass demobilization of the British Army. It was a politically nightmarish role. Already, some army units were on the brink of mutiny. Within a matter of months, Churchill had worked out what was widely accepted as an equitable and fair system for deciding who went home first.

The years of Liberal domination of British politics, however, were drawing to a close. In 1920, Churchill became Secretary of State for the Colonies but lost his seat two years later as the Liberals were swept from power. In 1924, however, he won election again when he rejoined the Conservatives and found himself Chancellor of the Exchequer.

When Andrew Dewar Gibb wrote *With Winston Churchill in the Trenches* that same year, Churchill's political career looked to have peaked.

Still, Gibb felt people were underestimating his old CO.

"We came to realize, to realize at first hand, his transcendent ability," he wrote. "He...left behind him there men who will always be his loyal partisans and admirers, and who are proud of having served in the Great War under the leadership of one who is beyond question a great man."

THE UNIT FORMED from the merger of the sixth and seventh battalions of the Royal Scots Fusiliers did itself survive the war. By February 1918, its losses had been so great it was first redesignated a "pioneer" battalion—responsible for trench maintenance and other administrative tasks—then reduced in size and abolished altogether.

Archie Sinclair—as he had wished—spent the rest of the conflict in the field. With the armistice, he returned to work for Churchill as a political aide. He served as Secretary of State for Air in the Second World War, ultimately almost resigning over his moral objections to the firebombing of Dresden.

Gibb returned to Edinburgh, resuming his legal practice but also entering politics. He was one of the founding members of the pro-independence Scottish National Party. Like many First World War veterans—including Churchill's old friend Jack Seely—he embraced a policy of appeasement to Nazi Germany and Fascist Italy in the 1930s. Eventually, he found himself sidelined through his own increasingly right-wing views.

The party he helped found, however, would have its day a century after his time in the trenches. In May 2015's general election the SNP swept the board in almost every Scottish constituency. Amongst those defeated were Archie Sinclair's grandson, then a Liberal Democrat MP. Churchill's old Dundee constituency too also fell.

Jock McDavid, Churchill's biographer Gilbert records, was hospitalized by a poison gas attack in 1918—the same year as Hitler—but made a relatively full recovery to work in the alcohol and beverage industry.

Edmund Hakewill-Smith remained in the Army, mostly with the Royal Scots Fusiliers. At the outbreak of war in 1939, he was a colonel. He was later promoted lieutenant-general, taking charge of the 52nd Lowland Division after D-Day. In early 1945, he became the first British general to set up headquarters inside Germany.

Most of Churchill's earlier contemporaries— those he had gone to Sandhurst with in particular— were gone.

"The South African War accounted for a large proportion...of my [earliest] friends," he had written in 1930. "The Great War killed almost all the others."

ON THE EVENING of May 9, 1940, Churchill dined in London with Sinclair—now Liberal party leader—and a handful of other close confidants. The next day, as he had expected, he was summoned to Buckingham Palace and asked to become prime minister. It was almost exactly twenty-five years since he had been thrown from Cabinet in 1915.

Churchill had been recalled to become First Lord of the Admiralty on September 3, 1939—the day before Chamberlain declared war on Germany. Throughout the first months of the war, he had agonized that history might repeat itself and he might once again be thrown from power just when it mattered.

Instead, he was taking the highest political office in the land at perhaps the country's most perilous moment.

In Europe, the military situation was collapsing by the hour. The same day he took office, May 10, German forces blasted into Holland and Belgium, overwhelming local resistance in a matter of hours. In France, the new British Expeditionary Force was in full retreat. The invasion of Britain, commanders believed, could follow almost immediately.

Churchill, though, later wrote that he felt more "a profound sense of relief." "At last I had the authority to give directions over the whole scene. I felt as though I was walking with destiny and that all my past life had been but a preparation."

To the public, he pledged "blood, toil, sweat and tears." To his police bodyguard, he privately admitted he feared it was too late to save the country.

Soon he was living once again under constant bombardment, this time in a fortified annex near Downing Street as German bombers blitzed the capital. Sometimes, as in 1916, he made his way to the top of a building in his tin hat and simply watched the battle.

It was a new tin hat—the original French helmet remained at Chartwell. At his side, however, he still carried the same pistol he had kept in the trenches.

Almost all of Churchill's top officials and contemporaries had been shaped by that earlier war. Clement Attlee, the Labour Party leader who became Churchill's deputy—and ultimately replacement—had

been one of the last officers off the beach at the
Dardanelles. He had never blamed Churchill for the
catastrophe and always felt he would be a good
national leader. Almost all his generals had been
junior officers in the trenches.

Churchill himself had spent a decade after the
First World War studying it, learning from what he
believed had been the mistakes. Now he tried to apply
those lessons.

That meant more direct control than Asquith
ever dreamed of. It also meant appointing senior
commanders—most notably Chief of the Imperial
General Alan Brooke—who would challenge him and
tell him he was wrong. Sometimes, those obsessions
caused chaos. At one stage, a fear of repeating
Gallipoli almost caused him to try and cancel D-Day.
But they kept him and those in power focused on
those at the sharp end in a way Churchill felt had
never happened a quarter century earlier.

By then, there was a new 6th Battalion Royal
Scots Fusiliers, badly mauled in the retreat to
Dunkirk. Churchill was to keep track of it throughout,
particularly as it fought its way across Europe as part
of Hakewill-Smith's division.

An undated War Office photo shows him
visiting them at barracks in northern England, a gas
mask case at his hip, addressing a cheering throng.

Some, he knew, would not survive.

"War is a game to be played with a smiling
face," Churchill wrote to his daughter Sarah in
November 1943. "But...I never forget the man at the
front, the bitter struggles and the fact that men are
dying.

THE END

PETER APPS

Select bibliography

With Winston Churchill at the Front, Capt X (Andrew Dewar Gibb), 1924

Winston S Churchill: The Biography (particularly Volume 3: The Challenge of War 1914-1916, Martin Gilbert, 1972

Churchill, a Life, Martin Gilbert, 1991

Winston S Churchill 3, supporting documents, Martin Gilbert, 1973

Speaking for Themselves: The Private Letters of Sir Winston and Clementine Churchill, edited by their daughter Mary Soames, 1999

Thoughts and Adventures, Winston S Churchill, 1932 (includes essays *With the Grenadiers* and *Plugstreet*)

The World Crisis, Winston S Churchill, 1923

My Early Life, Winston S. Churchill, 1930

Churchill: A Biography, Roy Jenkins, 2001

The Churchill Factor, Boris Johnson, 2015

The History of the Royal Scots Fusiliers (1678-1918), John Buchan, 1925

Liberal Crusader: The Life of Sir Archibald Sinclair, Gerald De Groot, 1993

First Lady: The Life and Wars of Clementine Churchill,
Sonia Purnell, 2015

Forgotten Victory, Gary Sheffield, 2001

About the Author

Peter Apps is global defence correspondent for Reuters news. In 2006, he broke his neck in a minibus accident while covering the civil war in Sri Lanka, leaving him largely paralyzed from the shoulders down. Of the 20 or so countries he has reported from, more than half have been since the injury. He is currently on sabbatical as Executive Director of the Project for Study of the 21st Century (PS21). Visit PS21 online at www.projects21.com.